475 basic wo

Desig

MW01242158

Additional 400

separate explanations or examples of using the words in sentences

Word origins — to make it easier to remember the words … and to build your vocabulary!

Many words are illustrated with caricatures!

Simple pronunciation shows how to pronounce the words

Each word is used in *several* sentences – to show various ways words can be used.

Sentences have clear and detailed punctuation – to help you learn English phrases and clauses.

Many sentences contain historical information – to make learning even more rewarding for you!

Famous Quotations by authors, scientists, and actors for all 475

words— so you can see how famous people use the words you are

learning!

Simple practice tests after every few words – to help you

remember and use the words in a sentence.

Also – 100 common English phrases (Many illustrated

with caricatures)

"My English Notes" in the back – blank pages to write down questions or words

Come in and see for yourself…

Professor Charles Says...
Learn English!

Charles W Sutherland

With Daniel C Sutherland

Illustrations by David Carter

Library of Congress Cataloging-in-Publication Data (forthcoming):

Sutherland, Charles W

ISBN-13: 978-1535460408
ISBN-10: 1535460407

Printed in the United States of America

First Edition

Author and creator: Charles W Sutherland
Contributing author and designer: Daniel C Sutherland
Illustrator: David Carter, Montgomery College Art Department

To students around the world who wish to learn, and to the parents and teachers in homes and schools around the world who help them

"Language is the oxygen of civilization. Without communication, society could not breathe and grow." – Professor Charles

Table of Contents

"Education is a wealth you
can never lose."

– Professor Charles

1.   a·ban·don [verb] From Old French *ad* ("at") + *bandon* ("power")— to give up power

Definition: To walk away

Usage:

The king ***abandoned*** his throne, and left the country.

When the tornado came, she had to ***abandon*** her home.

When the waves became too dangerous, the captain told his crew to ***abandon*** the ship.

Famous Quotation:

"My whole life I had the fear that I was going to be **abandoned**." – Halle Berry, American actress

2.   ab·duct [verb] From Latin *ab* ("away") + *ducere* ("to take")— to take away

Definition: To take someone away by force

Usage:

The kidnapper ***abducted*** the baby from its bedroom when the child was sleeping.

The villain ***abducted*** the girl and demanded that her parents pay him ransom money.

Famous Quotation:

"Sometimes I wish the aliens would ***abduct*** me and crown me as their leader." – George Noory, American television personality

Related words:

abduction   [noun] Kidnapping someone

abductor   [noun/person] Someone who kidnaps

3.   ac·cu·mu·late [verb] From Latin *accumulare* ("to heap up")— to pile up

Definition: To keep adding more and more

Usage:

She loved to ***accumulate*** souvenirs from the countries she had visited.

The professor ***accumulated*** papers from his former students and kept them.

"***Accumulate*** knowledge, and then understand what you learn by questioning."— Professor Charles

Related word:

accumulation [noun] A pile of things which have been collected.

4.   **ac·cu·rate** [adjective] From Latin *accuratus* ("prepared carefully")— preparing carefully

Definition: Without any mistakes

Usage:

He has to be very ***accurate*** in order to properly assemble all of the pieces of the clock.

When the student wrote her lessons, she was ***accurate*** and did not make any mistakes.

Famous Quotation:

"A stupid man's report of what a clever man says can never be ***accurate***, because he unconsciously translates what he hears into something he can understand." – Bertrand Russell, British philosopher and Nobel Laureate

Related word:

accuracy [noun] The status of being correct

5.   **ac·cuse** [verb] From Latin *accusare* ("to hold someone accountable")— to blame

Definition: To blame someone for doing something wrong

Usage:

The police ***accused*** the man of robbing a store.

The teacher ***accused*** the student of copying the answers of another student.

Famous Quotation:

"People ***accuse*** me of being arrogant all the time. I'm not arrogant; I'm focused." – Russell Crowe, Australian actor

Related words:

accusation [noun] The claim that someone did something wrong.

accused [noun/person] The person blamed for doing something wrong.

Match the word with the letter of the correct definition.

_____ abandon   (a) to keep adding more

_____ abduct   (b) correct

_____ accumulate   (c) to walk away

_____ accurate   (d) to charge someone with doing wrong

_____ accuse   (e) to take someone away by force

Fill in the blank with the best word. Each word will only be used once.

abandon   abduct   accumulate   accurate   accuse

(a)   The man decided to _____the little boy, and demand payment for his return.

(b)   Sheila called the police, and _____ the man of kidnapping.

(c)   The information Sheila provided was not _____ , and so it was not helpful.

(d)   The police needed to _____ more evidence, before they could arrest the man.

(e)   If the police could not get more evidence, they would have to_____ the case.

6. **ac·quire** [verb] From Latin *acquaerere* ("to add, or gain")— to get possession of

Definition: To get something

Usage:

The family wanted to *acquire* a new car for their son.

The medical student was studying hard to *acquire* her medical degree.

Famous Quotation:

"You can *acquire* a lot of knowledge without going to school." – Ron Glass, American actor

Related words:

acquisition [noun] The thing that you got

acquisitive [adjective] Having the desire to get things

7. **a·dapt** [verb] From Latin *adaptare* ("to adjust")— to make suitable

Definition: To adjust, or make suitable for some purpose

Usage:

He needed to *adapt* the car to meet the requirements of the automobile contest.

She wanted to *adapt* herself to her new surroundings in the school.

Famous Quotation:

"Intelligence is the ability to *adapt* to change." – Stephen Hawking, English theoretical physicist and cosmologist

Related words:

adaptable [adjective] Capable of changing

adaptation [noun] The act of changing something to fit its surroundings

8. **ad·dic·tion** [noun] From Latin *addicere* ("to give into, to yield")— to surrender to something

Definition: An uncontrollable need for something

Usage as a noun:

The young man had an *addiction* to cigarettes, and could not quit smoking.

The patient in the hospital developed an **addiction** to the pain medicine he was taking.

Famous Quotation:

"Every form of **addiction** is bad, whether the narcotic be alcohol, morphine, or idealism." – Carl Gustav Jung, Swiss psychiatrist and author

Related words:

addict [noun/person] Someone who has an uncontrollable need to have something.

addictive [adjective] The quality of something which makes it necessary to have it.

Usage as an adjective:

The doctors told her that cigarettes are **addictive**.

9. **ad·ja·cent** [adjective] From Latin *ad* ("to") + *iacere* ("to lie")— to lie near something

Definition: Immediately next to another thing

Usage:

The woman's house was **adjacent** to the large building.

The desks in the classroom were **adjacent** to each other, so that the students could share books.

Famous Quotation:

"We only included patients whose cancers had not invaded **adjacent** organs." – Dr. Jaap Bonjer, Dutch Professor of Surgery

10. **ad·o·les·cent** [noun/ person] From Latin *ad* ("to") +*alescere* ("to nourish")— developing

Definition: A young person who has not yet become an adult

Usage:

The young man was just beginning to grow his beard, because he was an **adolescent**.

The girl wanted to become a fully-grown woman, and not be an **adolescent** any longer.

Famous Quotation:

"The day a child realizes that all adults are not perfect, he becomes an *adolescent*. The day he forgives them, he becomes an adult." – Alden Nowlan, Canadian poet and playwright

Related word:

adolescence [noun] The stage in life of being a young person, still not an adult

Match the word with the letter of the correct definition.

_____ acquire	(a) to make something suitable
_____ adapt	(b) something nearby
_____ addiction	(c) to gain through effort
_____ adjacent	(d) a young person
_____ adolescent	(e) an uncontrollable need

Fill in the blank with the best word. Each word will only be used once.

acquire   adapt   addiction   adjacent   adolescent

(a)   Helen's father had to go to the hospital because of his
_____ to cigarettes.

(b)   Helen wanted to become an adult, but she was still an
_____.

(c)   She needed to earn more money before she could
_____ a new car.

(d)   When Helen moved to a different country, it took time for her
to _____ to her new environment.

(e)   She enjoyed her new neighbors in the house _____
to her house.

From the 1930's, when speakers or actors would secretly read from notes they made on the disposable paper cuffs of their shirt sleeves.

11.   ad·ver·sar·y [noun/person] From Latin *ad ("to") + vertere* ("to turn")— someone against you

Definition: Someone against you

Usage:

The strongest *adversary* of the football team was the team they had often played against.

The boxer had to fight an *adversary* who was much bigger than he was.

Famous Quotation:

"With wolves around, your humility is your worst *adversary*." – Pawan Mishra, Indian author

Related words:

adversarial [adjective] Having a relationship with someone who is against you

adversity [noun] A state of hardship or misfortune when events are against you.

adverse [adjective] Something or someone who is opposed to your interests

adversely [adverb] When actions or events are going against you

12.   ad·vo·cate [verb, noun/person] From Latin *ad ("to") vocare* ("to call")— to speak for someone

Definition: To speak positively for someone

Usage:

The lawyer wanted to *advocate* for his client, and persuade the judge that she was innocent.

It was important for the principal to *advocate* for those students who needed scholarships in order to continue in school.

Famous Quotation:

"No man should *advocate* in private what he is ashamed to *advocate* in public." – George McGovern, American Senator

Usage as a noun:

She was the best *advocate* the girls could have for their cause.

13.   aes·thet·ic [adjective] From Greek *aisthetikos* ("sensitive" or "perceptive")— feeling good

Definition: Appreciating beauty

Usage:

He valued her *aesthetic* appreciation of the paintings in the museum.

The entire experience of listening to the classical music was an *aesthetic* delight.

Famous Quotation:

"Nature holds the key to our *aesthetic*, intellectual, cognitive, and even spiritual satisfaction." – E.O. Wilson, American biologist and author

Related words:

aesthetics [noun] The study of the nature of beauty

aesthete [noun/ person] Someone who has a deep appreciation of beauty

14.   af·fec·tion [noun] From Latin *affectionem* ("emotional feeling")— a tender feeling

Definition: A feeling of tenderness or fondness

Usage:

She has much *affection* for her classmates.

The dogs acted like they had *affection* for each other.

Famous Quotation:

"You are the object of my *affection*." – A song

Related word:

affectionate [adjective] Having tender feelings for someone or something.

15.   af·flu·ent [adjective] From Latin *affluentia* ("a flowing toward" ... apparently since flowing water ... and money ... produced health and prosperity)—flowing over with money

Definition: To be wealthy

Usage:

The *affluent* family took vacations in different countries every year.

To be *affluent* does not mean to be happy, but it helps.

Famous Quotation:

"The only *affluent* are those who do not want more than they have." –
Erich Fromm, German psychologist and philosopher

Related word:

affluence [noun] Wealth

Match the word with the letter of the correct definition.

_____ adversary	(a) appreciating beauty
_____ advocate	(b) someone against you
_____ aesthetic	(c) a feeling of tenderness
_____ affection	(d) being wealthy
_____ affluent	(e) to speak for someone

Fill in the blank with the best word. Each word will only be used once.

adversary   advocate   aesthetic   affection   affluent

(a)   Elizabeth hired a good lawyer to be her _____ in
the court.

(b)   Elizabeth faced a powerful _____ in her legal
fight.

(c)   Elizabeth was not _____ , so she needed
financial help.

(d)   One of her friends had much _____ for her, and was
willing to help.

(e)   She and her friend shared an _____ appreciation for
art.

16. ag·gra·vate [verb] From Latin *ad* ("to") + *gravare* ("to weigh down")— to become a burden
Definition: To annoy, or disturb
Usage:
The boys tried to **aggravate** their opponents by calling them names.
The woman **aggravated** the dog by spraying water on it.
Famous Quotation:
"Nothing **aggravates** angry people more than when you are calm when they are angry." – Professor Charles
Related word:
aggravation [noun] The state of being annoyed or aggravated

17. ag·gre·gate [verb, noun] From Latin *ad* ("to") + *gregare* ("a herd")— add to the herd
Definition: To add together
Usage as a verb:
The farmer decided to **aggregate** all of the sheep into one large flock.
The store owner wanted to **aggregate** all of his food products into one part of the store.
Usage as a noun:
Human wisdom is the **aggregate** of all human experience.
Famous Quotation:
"The world is moved along, not only by the mighty shoves of its heroes, but also by the **aggregate** of tiny pushes of each honest worker." – Helen Keller, blind-mute author

18. ag·nos·tic [noun/person] From Greek *a* ("not")+ *gnostos* ("knowable")— someone who does not know
Definition: Someone who claims nothing can be known about the existence of God.
Usage:
He is an **agnostic**, and does not believe in the teachings of any religion.
She studied philosophy to find out the difference between an **agnostic** and an atheist.

"Confucius was a humanist, and an *agnostic*." – Hu Shih, Chinese philosopher and writer

Related word:

agnosticism [noun] The philosophy that one cannot prove there is a God.

19.   al·le·giance [noun] From Anglo-French *legaunce* "(loyalty of a liege to his lord")—loyalty to someone of a superior rank

Definition: Loyalty to a person, a country or a cause

Usage:

He professed his *allegiance* to the king.

The government requested that the soldiers pledge their *allegiance* to the country.

Famous Quotation:

"Our country is not the only thing to which we owe our *allegiance*. It is also owed to justice and to humanity." – James Bryce, Irish naturalist and writer

20.   al·lo·cate [verb] From Latin *ad* ("to") + *locare* ("the place")—to put in different places

Definition: To put in separate places

Usage:

The university president *allocated* most of the money to the library and to the laboratories.

The president *allocated* the responsibility to a team of three people.

The general decided to *allocate* most of his troops to the main battle field.

Famous Quotation:

"Millions of individuals making their own decisions in the marketplace will always *allocate* resources better than any centralized government planning." – Ronald Reagan, American president

Related word:

allocation [noun] The result of putting things into separate places

Match the word with the letter of the correct definition.

_____ aggravate   (a) to be loyal

_____ aggregate   (b) to annoy or disturb

_____ agnostic   (c) to add things together

_____ allegiance   (d) does not know if God exists

_____ allocate   (e) to put in separate places

Fill in the blank with the best word. Each word will only be used once.

aggravate   aggregate   agnostic   allegiance   allocate

(a)   As the new coach, Clay wanted to demonstrate his
_____ to the school.

(b)   When the players did not know the school's history, Clay
became _____ .

(c)   Clay had questions for the players, because he was
_____about their backgrounds.

(d)   Clay decided to _____ the new uniforms to the best
players.

(e)   The total number of players now began to _____into
a large group.

21.   am·bi·dex·trous [adjective]   From Latin *ambi* ("both") + *dexter* ("on the right" or "right hand")—   literally, 'two/both right hands'

Definition: Physical ability to use both hands equally well.

Usage:

Because she is ***ambidextrous***, she can write equally well with both hands.

He can use both hands equally well, since he is ***ambidextrous***.

Famous Quotation:

"I'm ***ambidextrous***. I can write just as poorly with either hand." – Jarod Kintz, American writer

Related Word:

ambidexterity [noun] The quality of being able to use both hands equally well.

22.   am·big·u·ous [adjective]   From Latin *ambiguus (*"two meanings"*)* from *ambi ("both") + agere (*"to wander")— "to go both ways"

Definition: Open to more than one interpretation. Confusing or perplexing.

Usage:

The politician's statement was ***ambiguous***; so no one knew for sure what he meant.

She promised to help him, but the way she said it was very ***ambiguous***.

Famous Quotation:

"Real politics is messy and morally ***ambiguous***..." – James Surowieski, American writer

Related word:

ambiguity [noun] The condition of being unclear and confusing

23.   a·mend [verb]   From Latin *emendare* ("to correct")—to improve

Definition: To change for the better, or to correct errors

Usage:

He decided to **amend** his writings, so that they were easier for people to read.

The people decided to **amend** the Constitution, in order to include more provisions for voting.

Related words:

amends [noun] Something given to you to repay you for an injury

amendment [noun] The result of changing something, for example, an Amendment to the Constitution.

Famous Quotation:

The First **Amendment** [freedom of speech] has the same role in my life as a citizen and a writer as the sun has in our ecosystem." – Michael Chabon, American author

24.   a·nal·y·sis From Greek *ana* ("up") + *lysis* ("loosen")—loosen into parts

Definition: To separate an idea into parts to examine it

Usage:

His **analysis** of the issues was correct, and it helped him decide what to do.

The general asked his staff to provide him with an **analysis** of the battlefield situation.

Famous Quotation:

"When a truth is necessary, the reason for it can be found in **analysis**, that is, by resolving it into simpler ideas and truths until the primary ones are discovered." – Gottfried Leibniz, German mathematician and philosopher

Related words:

analyze [verb] To provide a detailed examination of something

analytic [adjective] Having the quality of performing detailed examinations

25.   an·ces·tor [noun/person] From Latin *ante* ("before") + *cedere* ("to go")— a predecessor

Definition: Someone who went before you, either a grandparent or someone in your country.

Usage:

The **ancestors** of the British people lived hundreds of years ago.

She wants to know who the **ancestors** in her family are.

Famous Quotation:

"We must strive to become good **ancestors**." — Ralph Nader, American political activist and writer

Related words:

ancestry [noun/people] All of the people in your past

ancestral [adjective] Something pertaining to the people in your past

Match the word with the letter of the correct definition.

_____ ambidextrous	(a) to change
_____ ambiguous	(b) having two meanings
_____ amend	(c) someone who lived before you
_____ analysis	(d) to use both hands equally well
_____ ancestor	(e) to break an idea apart

Please fill in the blank with the best word. Each word will only be used once!

ambiguous   ambidextrous   amend   analysis   ancestor

(a)   Charline decided she had to _____ her paper, if she wanted to get a good grade.

(b)   Charline could write equally well with either hand, because she was _____ .

(c)   She studied the history of her family and was proud to have such a wonderful _____ .

(d)   She had to perform a careful _____ to understand the ideas involved.

(e)   She never knew for sure what the lawyer meant, because his words were so _____.

26.   an·nex [noun, verb] From Old French *annexer* ("additional building")—to add or attach

Definition: Adding to a building, or to a country

Usage as a noun:

To make the building larger, the owner of the building built an ***annex***.

To expand their house, the family built an ***annex***.

Usage as a verb:

To expand his country, the dictator decided to ***annex*** part of the neighboring country.

Famous Quotation:

"I would ***annex*** the planets if I could. I often think of that. It makes me sad to see them so clear and yet so far away." – Cecil Rhodes, British explorer

Related words:

annexation [noun] The process of adding something

27.   an·tic·i·pate [verb] From Latin *anti* ("before") + *capere* ("to take")— to realize earlier

Definition: To be aware in advance

Usage:

He ***anticipated*** that his friend would arrive earlier than planned.

She could not ***anticipate*** what would happen after the speech.

The students ***anticipated*** the test would be very difficult.

Famous Quotation:

"***Anticipate*** the difficult, by managing the easy things." – Lao Tsu, Chinese philosopher

Related word:

anticipation [noun] The act of being aware of what will happen

28.   ap·pre·hend [verb] From Latin *ad* ("to") + *prehendere* ("to seize")— to seize

Definition: To seize someone in the name of the law; to understand something

Usage:

The police *apprehended* the bank robber an hour after he stole the money.

She studied hard, and was able to *apprehend* the information.

Famous Quotation:

"Intelligence is being quick to *apprehend*, which is distinct from ability, which is the capacity to act wisely on the thing that was *apprehended*." – Alfred North Whitehead, American mathematician and philosopher

Related words:

apprehensive [adjective] Fearful about the future

apprehension [noun] The ability to understand; having fear about the future;

Usage as noun:

He was full of *apprehension,* when he anticipated how difficult the test would be.

29. ar·bi·trar·y [adjective] From Latin *arbitrarius* ("uncertain")— by chance

Definition: Decided by chance, not by reason

Usage:

The decisions of the dictator were *arbitrary*, since he did whatever he felt like doing.

The decision of the judge was *arbitrary*, because it depended upon which lawyer he liked the most.

Famous Quotation:

"*Arbitrary* power is most easily established on the ruins of liberty." – George Washington, first American president

Related words:

arbitration [noun] Presenting a dispute to someone else to judge, and not knowing what the decision will be

arbitrator [noun/person] The person who makes the decision

30. ar·ro·gance [noun] From Latin *arrogare* ("to claim for oneself")— unjustified claims about yourself

Definition: Excessively proud; claiming to be more important than you really are

Usage:

Most people avoided him because of his ***arrogance*** in dealing with others.

She loved him, but was always annoyed by his ***arrogance***.

Famous Quotation:

"False modesty can be worse than ***arrogance***." – David Mitchell, English writer

Related word:

arrogant [adjective] The quality of being too proud

Match the word with the letter of the correct definition.

_____ annex	(a) to seize someone or something
_____ anticipate	(b) excessively proud
_____ apprehend	(c) to add on
_____ arbitrary	(d) to expect something before it happens
_____ arrogance	(e) decided by chance

Fill in the blank with the best word. Each word will only be used once.

annex   anticipate   apprehend   arbitrary   arrogance

(a)   When talking about his large house, Bill always displayed his

_____ .

(b)   To make his house even larger, Bill decided to build an

_____ .

(c)   Bill found it difficult to _____ all of the information the builder told him.

(d)   Bill wanted to be careful, and not make an _____ decision.

(e)   Bill calculated the various items to be purchased, and tried to _____ the final cost.

31. as·cer·tain [verb] From Latin *a* ("to") + *certus* ("certain") — to make certain.

Definition: To discover facts

Usage:

The scholar had to *ascertain* what exactly happened several hundred years ago.

The police wanted to *ascertain* the name of the person in the car.

Famous Quotation:

"Science can *ascertain* what is, but not what should be." – Albert Einstein, American scientist

32. as·sess [verb] From Latin *assessare* ("to fix a tax upon")— to place a value on

Definition: To evaluate something

Usage:

The tax collector had to *assess* the value of every house on the street.

The general had to *assess* the strength of the opposing army.

Related words:

asset [noun] Something of value

assessment [noun] The value that was determined

Famous Quotation:

"I made my own **assessment** of my life, and I began to live it. That was freedom." – Fernando Flores, Chilean engineer and politician

33. as·sim·i·late [verb] From Latin *ad* ("to") + *simulare* ("make similar")— to make similar

Definition: To bring together, and to make a part of something

Usage:

The students had to *assimilate* all of the material which the professor gave them to study.

The government made plans to *assimilate* the immigrants into the population.

Famous Quotation:

"I have deliberately studied many things that I know I won't be able to *assimilate*. I read Plato, St. Thomas, the mystics, to exercise my mind." – Don Ameche, American actor

Related word:

assimilation [noun] The result of bringing things or people together

34.   as·so·ci·a·tion [noun] From Latin *associare* "(to join with")—
to become a group
Definition: A group of people who have joined together for some
purpose
Usage:
She joined an ***association*** of all girls who were interested in learning
about the history of American women.
The Boy Scouts of America is an ***association*** of over 2,000,000 boys
which was created in 1910.
Famous Quotation:
"Successful people carefully manage their energy and ***associations***." –
Bryant McGill, American author
Related words:
associate [noun/person] Someone who is part of a group
associate [verb] To join with another person or other people
Usage as verb:
She wanted to ***associate*** with the girls in the art class.

35.   as·tron·o·my [noun]From Greek *astron* ("star") + *nomos*
("arrangement")—study of the stars
Definition: The study of the stars and the universe
Usage:
She was a professor of ***astronomy***, and had studied the stars for over
ten years.
Once he studied ***astronomy***, he looked at the world differently.
Famous Quotation:
"***Astronomy*** compels the soul to look upwards, and leads us from this
world to another." – Plato, Greek philosopher
Related words:
astronomical [adjective] Something related to the stars
astronomer [noun/person] Someone who studies the stars and
planets
astronaut [noun/ person] Someone who travels into space to see the
stars and planets
astrology [noun] The study of the location of stars and planets with the
belief that they affect human decisions

Match the word with the letter of the correct definition.

_____ ascertain   (a) to digest and make part of you

_____ assess   (b) to discover facts

_____ assimilate   (c) study of the stars

_____ association   (d) to evaluate

_____ astronomy   (e) a group with the same purpose

Fill in the blank with the best word. Each word will only be used once.

ascertain   assess   assimilate   association   astronomy

(a)   It was difficult to _____ how much damage had been done by the storm.

(b)   Even as a child Nate loved to look at the stars. So it was no surprise when he began to study _____ .

(c)   There were so many different stories from the witnesses, that it was difficult for the police to _____ the truth of what happened.

(d)   The alumni of the college created their own _____ , so they could remain in communication with each other.

(e)   It was difficult for someone from Europe to _____ into the culture of Asia.

Professor Charles Explains

Why We Say: *Chew the Fat*

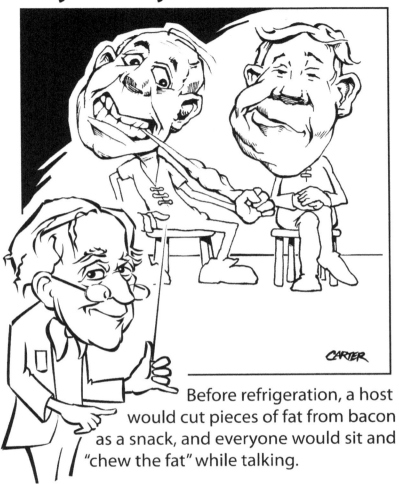

CARTER

Before refrigeration, a host would cut pieces of fat from bacon as a snack, and everyone would sit and "chew the fat" while talking.

36.   au·thor·i·ty [noun, noun/person] From Latin *auctor* ("master")—power to enforce laws

Definition: The power to make decisions affecting other people, or to enforce laws

Usage as a noun:

The judge has the ***authority*** to send someone to prison if they commit a crime.

The principal used his ***authority*** to tell the students they have to stay in the library to study.

Famous Quotation:

"Moral ***authority*** comes from following universal and timeless principals like honesty, integrity, and treating people with respect."– Stephen Covey, American educator

Usage as a person:

The professor is an ***authority*** on the subject of European history.

Related words:

authorize [verb] To give power to someone for some purpose

author [noun/person] Someone with knowledge on a particular subject

37.   au·ton·o·my [noun] From Greek *autonomia* ("independence")— independent

Definition: The condition of being independent

Usage:

The new country enjoyed its ***autonomy***, since it had sought its independence for a long time.

With his new ***autonomy*** from his parents, the young man was not sure what he should do.

Famous Quotation:

"[People] lose their social freedom and their individual ***autonomy*** in seeking to become like each other." – David Riesman, American sociologist

Related word:

autonomous [adjective] Having freedom and not being controlled by others

38.   av·er·age [noun] From Arabic *arwariya* ("equal sharing… of loss from shipments")—an intermediate number

Definition: Something in the middle, between two extremes

Usage:

The *average* height of the students was five feet and six inches.
The cars travelled at an *average* speed of 55 miles per hour on the highway.
Famous Quotation:
"Great minds discuss ideas; *average* minds discuss events; small minds discuss people." –
Eleanor Roosevelt, American humanist and wife of President Franklin D. Roosevelt

39.   a·ver·sion [noun] From Latin *a* ("from") + *vertere* ("to turn")— turn away from
Definition: Turning away from something, or to have a strong dislike of something
Usage:
He is a very quiet person, and so he has an *aversion* to crowds.
She has a strong *aversion* to alcohol, and stays away from people who drink a lot.
Famous Quotation:
"I've always had an *aversion* to debt."– Brunello Cucinelli, Italian fashion designer
Related word:
avert [verb] To turn away from something
Usage as a verb:
She drove the car away from the boy playing in the street, in order to **avert** a tragedy.

40.   bal·ance [verb, noun] From Latin *bilanx* ("scale")— equality of totals
Definition: Of equal weight; to make things equal
Usage as a verb:
The scale was invented to measure the *balance* between two different things.
She had to *balance* the amount of time she needed for study and the time she had to work.
It was hard for him to **balance** all of the responsibilities that were required of him.
Usage as a noun:
The teachers were trying to have the right *balance* between work and play.
Famous Quotation:

"Nature is consistently striving for *balance.*" – Joseph Rain, American writer

Match the word with the letter of the correct definition.

_____ authority	(a) being independent
_____ autonomy	(b) to turn away from
_____ average	(c) the power to make decisions
_____ aversion	(d) weighing something
_____ balance	(e) something ordinary

Fill in the blank with the best word. Each word will only be used once.

authority   autonomy   average   aversion   balance

(a)   Betty had no particular strength or skills, since she was just an_____ girl.

(b)   Betty finally had the _____ to lead her own life.

(c)   The government leaders have the _____to repair the roads when they are broken.

(d)   Betty had an _____ to certain nuts, since they gave her a rash on her skin.

(e)   It was difficult for Betty to _____the responsibilities of a career and being a mother.

41.   beau·ti·ful [adjective] From Latin *bellus* ("pretty")— having qualities that delight the senses
Definition: Something pleasing to look at
Usage:
She sat on the beach, and watched the ***beautiful*** sunrise in the morning.
Whenever he looks at her, he admires how ***beautiful*** she is.
Famous Quotation:
"The best and most ***beautiful*** things in the world cannot be seen or even touched—they must be felt with the heart." – Helen Keller, American blind-mute author
Related word:
beauty [noun] [sometimes a person] Something or someone who is nice to look at

42.   bi·as [noun] From French *biais* ("slant")—a slant
Definition: A slanted opinion (for or against) someone or something before you have any facts
Usage:
Whenever he watched a soccer game, he had a ***bias*** in favor of his home team.
She had a ***bias*** toward girls, and always gave them more opportunities than she gave boys.
Famous Quotation:
"Science is the search for truth, and an effort to understand the world. It involves the rejection of ***bias***, of dogma, of revelation, but not the rejection of morality." – Linus Pauling, American chemist and biochemist
Related word:
biased [adjective] Having an opinion before knowing the facts

43.   bib·li·og·ra·phy [noun] From Greek *biblio* ("book") + *graphos* ("writing")— list of books
Definition: A list of books
Usage:
At the end of her college paper, she wrote a ***bibliography*** of the books she used in her research.
He wrote a **bibliography** of all the books he read while he was in college.
Famous Quotation:

"A student should learn something about field work, something about *bibliography*, and something about how to carry out library research."
– Alan Dundes, American educator and author
Related word:
bible [noun] A book

44.   bi·ol·o·gy [noun] From Greek *bios* ("life") + *logia* ("study")— the study of life
Definition: The study of life and living organisms
Usage:
She obtained her college degree in *biology*, because she wanted to become a medical doctor.
The professor of *biology* explained the lives of different animals.
Famous Quotation:
"I am very comfortable with the idea that we can override *biology* with free will." – Richard Dawkins, British biologist and author
Related words:
biological [adjective] Related to the study of the body
biopsy [noun] Removing some tissue from a body to examine it

45.   blame [verb, noun] From Modern French *blâmer* ("condemn")— to hold responsible
Definition: To find fault, or hold someone responsible
Usage as a verb:
The mother *blamed* the neighbor boy for stepping on the flowers in her garden.
She tried to *blame* other people for everything that went wrong in her life.
Famous Quotation:
"A person who always *blames* destiny for everything in his life is the person who can never succeed in life." – Anurag Prakash Ray, Indian author
Usage as a noun:
The man received the *blame* for causing the fire.
Related word:
blameworthy [adjective] Guilty of doing something wrong

Match the word with the letter of the correct definition.

_____ beautiful   (a) a list of books
_____ bias   (b) nice to look at
_____ bibliography   (c) to condemn someone
_____ biology   (d) an opinion not based on facts
_____ blame   (e) the study of living things

Fill in the blank with the best word. Each word will only be used once.

beautiful   bias   bibliography   biology   blame

(a)   Cristin decided to study _____ , so she could become a health practitioner.

(b)   Since the lady became obese by eating too much, no one else could be _____ .

(c)   Cristin ate healthy foods, and so she remained _____ even when she was older.

(d)   Cristin assembled a large _____ of books to use for her research.

(e)   It was natural for Cristin to have a _____ in favor of her brother's football team.

46.   bor·ing [adjective] From Old English *bore* ("tiring")—
uninteresting
Definition: Tiresome and not interesting
Usage:
Her long speech was so ***boring*** that everyone fell asleep.
The play was so ***boring*** that people were happy when it was over.
Famous Quotation:
"Life can be ***boring*** unless you put some effort into it." – John C.
Maxwell, American author
Related word:
bore [noun/person] Someone who is not interesting

47.   bon·fire [noun] A fire with friends.
Definition: A friendly neighborhood fire with friends
Usage:
They had a ***bonfire*** on the beach, and cooked hotdogs under the stars.
After their spring cleaning, the couple burned many of their old clothes
in a large ***bonfire***.
Famous Quotation:
"Desire is a ***bonfire*** that burns with greater fury, asking for more fuel."
– Sia Sathya Sai Baba, India, guru

48.   boy·cott [verb, noun] (From 19th century Ireland, when
tenants refused to work on farms managed by Charles C. Boycott
because of his actions.)— a refusal to do business with someone
Definition: To refuse to work, or refuse to buy and sell products to a
company or country.
Usage as a verb:
The angry people decided to ***boycott*** the company and not buy any
more of its products.
Usage as a noun:
Many countries created an economic ***boycott*** of Iran, and would not
buy Iranian oil.
Famous Quotation:
"The main problem is that for a ***boycott*** to be effective, you must first
persuade thousands – maybe even millions of others – to go along,

which is a lot of work and usually not successful." -- L. Neil. Smith, American author

49. bur·den [noun] From Old English *byroen* ("heavy weight")— something heavy to carry
Definition: Something heavy to carry, or difficult to emotionally bear
Usage:
The man had to carry a heavy *burden* of food all the way up the mountain.
Because of their ability to carry heavy loads, mules are called 'beasts of *burden*.'
The *burden* of managing the entire company fell on his shoulders.
Famous Quotation:
"The *burden* which is carried well becomes light." – Ovid, Greek philosopher
Related word:
burden of proof [noun] The heavy weight of responsibility to provide the evidence needed to convict someone in a court of law

50. bu·reauc·ra·cy [noun] From French *bureau* ("office, or desk") + Greek *kratia* ("power")— administration of a government
Definition: The administration offices of a government
Usage:
The *bureaucracy* became so large that no one had the authority to do anything.
He tried to implement some policies, but he could not get the *bureaucracy* to act.
Famous Quotation:
"*Bureaucracy*, the rule of no one, has become the modern form of despotism." – Mary McCarthy, American author
Related word:
bureaucrat [noun/person] Someone who works in a government office

Professor Charles Explains
Why We Say: *Bonfire*

Bones from animals eaten during the winter were pulled outside of homes, and were burned in a friendly "***bonefire***" to celebrate spring.

Match the word with the letter of the correct definition.

_____ boring	(a) something heavy to carry
_____ bonfire	(b) to refuse to buy something
_____ boycott	(c) something that makes you tired
_____ burden	(d) a fire with friends
_____ bureaucracy	(e) a government administration

Fill in the blank with the best word. Each word will only be used once.

boring   bonfire   burden   bureaucracy   boycott

(a)   To provide for a family of six children was a financial _____ for the parents.

(b)   Erica tried to avoid the people during coffee break, since their conversations were so _____ .

(c)   It was difficult for the president to change the nation's economic policies, because of the huge _____ that had to put his changes into action.

(d)   Erica decided to have a _____ and get rid of all of her old clothes.

(e)   The entire city decided to _____ the store because of the high price of its food.

51.   bur·y [verb] From Old English *byrgan* ("to hide")— to hide
Definition: To cover with dirt, or hide under other materials
Usage:
When their father died, they had to ***bury*** him in the cemetery.
He was ***buried*** under a pile of work that he had to finish.
Famous Quotation:
"Don't ***bury*** your thoughts. Put your vision to reality." – Bob Marley, Jamaican musician
Related word:
burial [noun] The act of covering something or someone

52.   can·did [adjective] From Latin *candidum* ("white, pure, honest")— free from prejudice
Definition: Honest when saying something
Usage:
He was always ***candid*** when he told the audience his opinions.
When someone is ***candid***, many people are upset with hearing the truth.
Famous Quotation:
"Be ***candid*** with everyone." – Jack Welch, American businessman, former CEO of General Electric
Related word:
candor [noun] Being open and honest

53.   can·di·date [noun/person] Latin *candidatus* ("white robed"... office seekers in ancient Rome wore white robes to show they were honest.) — someone seeking political office
Definition: Someone who wants to be elected to a position
Usage:
There were many ***candidates*** who wanted to be president.
The ***candidate*** traveled across the entire country, trying to get people to vote for him.
Famous Quotation:
"Every now and then, a presidential ***candidate*** surprises us with a truly human and honest moment." – Ron Fournier, American journalist
Related word:
candidacy [noun] Being in the process of seeking to be elected

54. car·tel [noun] From Middle French *cartel* ("a written agreement between two or more parties")— a combination of business organizations or countries

Definition: A group of countries or companies that join together to establish markets and fix prices for their products

Usage:

The petroleum-producing countries banded together to create a ***cartel***, in order to fix the price of oil.

The companies formed a ***cartel*** and offered higher prices for their products.

Famous Quotation:

"We must not tolerate oppressive governments or industrial oligarchy in the form of monopolies and ***cartels***." – Henry A. Wallace, American author

55. cast [verb, noun] From Old Norse *kasta* ("to throw")— to throw

Definition: To throw something

Usage as a verb:

"***Cast*** your bread upon the water" is a quotation from the Bible, Ecclesiastes 11.

He ***cast*** his fishing line into the water in order to catch some fish.

Famous Quotation:

"The world is a stage, but the players are badly ***cast***."— Oscar Wilde, Irish author

Usage as a noun:

The doctor put a ***cast*** on his broken arm to keep the bones straight.

One of her favorite movie stars was in the ***cast*** of the new movie.

Match the word with the letter of the correct definition.

_____ bury   (a) someone who wants to be elected

_____ candid   (b) honest

_____ candidate   (c) to cover or put into the ground

_____ cartel   (d) to throw something

_____ cast   (e) a group that joins together

Fill in the blank with the best word. Each word will only be used once.

bury   candid   candidate   cartel   cast

(a)   Julie was the most recent _____ running for the office of president.

(b)   The large building _____ a huge shadow over the entire street.

(c)   Julie decided to _____ her past mistakes, and never discuss them again.

(d)   The oil countries refused to allow some smaller countries into their _____ .

(e)   Julie was very _____ , when she told her boss that he was doing a bad job.

56.   ca·tas·tro·phe [adjective] From Greek *kata* ("down") + *strephein* ("to turn quickly")—a sudden calamity
Definition: Something that turned very bad quickly; a major disaster
Usage:
The fire was a ***catastrophe*** and burned down their entire house.
The tornado caused a ***catastrophe*** for the whole city.
Famous Quotation:
"Human history becomes more and more a race between education and ***catastrophe***." – H. G. Wells, English author
Related word:
catastrophic [adjective] Concerning a situation when something very bad happens

57.   cause [noun, verb] From Latin *causa* ("the reason")— the direct reason something happens
Definition: The reason something happens
Usage as a noun:
The boys were playing with matches, and that was the ***cause*** of the big fire.
His hard work was the main ***cause*** of his success.
Usage as a verb:
The hurricane ***caused*** damage to all of the houses on the beach.
Famous Quotation:
"Some people ***cause*** happiness *wherever* they go. Others ***cause*** happiness *whenever* they go." – Oscar Wilde, Irish author

58.   cease [verb] From Old French *cesser* ("to come to an end") – to stop
Definition: To stop
Usage:
The teacher told the children to ***cease*** making so much noise.
They had to ***cease*** playing outside because it began to rain.
Famous Quotation:
"Develop a passion for learning. If you do, you will never ***cease*** to grow." – Anthony J. D'Angelo, American educator
Related word:
cessation [noun] The condition of something that has stopped

Usage as a noun:
The war stopped; so there was a **cessation** of fighting.

59.   cer·ti·fy [verb] From Latin *certus* ("certain") + *facere* ("to make")— to make certain
Definition: To make certain, or verify the accuracy
Usage as verb:
The doctor had to ***certify*** that the patient needed the medicine.
The lawyer ***certified*** that the man was the real owner of the property.
Related word:
certificate [noun] An official document which makes certain that something is accurate and true
Usage as a noun:
She received a **certificate** from the school that she had passed the examinations.
Famous Quotation:
"In the early days of Indian Territory, there was no such thing as birth **certificates**. You being there was **certificate** enough." – Mark Twain, American author

60.   char·ac·ter·is·tic [noun] From Greek *kharakter* ("engraved mark")— a special mark
Definition: An individual trait
Usage:
The stripes on the zebra are its most unusual ***characteristic***.
The boy had a ***characteristic*** laugh which everyone knew.
Famous Quotation:
"It is a ***characteristic*** of wisdom not to do desperate things." – Henry David Thoreau, American author and philosopher
Related word:
character [noun] Qualities which belong to a particular person

Match the word with the letter of the correct definition.

_____ catastrophe	(a) to stop
_____ cause	(b) something very bad
_____ cease	(c) an individual trait
_____ certify	(d) the reason for something
_____ characteristic	(e) to make certain

Fill in the blank with the best word. Each word will only be used once.

catastrophe   cause   cease   certify   characteristic

(a)   The rain was the main _____ of Scott's car accident.

(b)   Due to the accident, the police had to _____ all driving on the road.

(c)   Although there was a great deal of damage, it was not a complete _____ .

(d)   The policeman wanted to _____ that Scott had a driver's license.

(e)   The policeman had the unusual _____ of bright blue eyes.

Why We Say: *Cold Feet*

One explanation is a 'fear response' can cause hyperventilation, slowing the blood flow to the extremities, causing "cold feet" and temporary paralysis.

61.   choose [verb] From Old English *ceosan* ("seek, decide")—to decide, or to select

Definition: To decide from a number of alternatives

Usage:

She had to *choose* between two different men who were in love with her.

When he went to vote, he did not know which candidate to *choose*.

Famous Quotation:

"*Choose* a job you love, and you will never have to work a day in your life." – Confucius, Chinese philosopher

Related word:

choice [noun] The item or person that someone preferred

62.   chro·nol·o·gy [noun] From Greek *kronos* ("time") + *logia* ("study")— a record of times

Definition: A record of different times when things happen

Usage:

The professor listed the *chronology* of the different wars in European history.

The captain of the ship mapped out the *chronology* of when the ship would arrive at each port.

Famous Quotation:

"You can study *chronology*, but that does not mean that you will use your time well." – Professor Charles

Related word:

chronological [adjective] Having to do with planning the use of time

63.   cir·cu·late [verb] From Latin *circulatus* ("to move around in a circle")— to move in a circle

Definition: To move around from place to place

Usage:

Since she was new on the college campus, she decided to *circulate* and meet people.

The marketing manager began to *circulate* the literature to the company's customers.

Famous Quotation:
"Knowledge is like money: to be of value, it must *circulate*." – Louis L'Amour, American writer

Related word:
circulation [noun] The movement of something, whether blood through the body, water through pipes, or printed material through the public

Usage as a noun:
The **circulation** of the blood through our body is one of the things that keep our bodies healthy.

When they added a Sports Section, the newspaper's **circulation** increased.

64.   civ·il [adjective] From Latin *civilis* ("relating to a citizen")— concerning citizens

Definition: Polite behavior among citizens

Usage:
It was a *civil* law suit regarding property, not a criminal process concerning some crime.

When speaking to each other, the two opposing politicians were both very *civil*.

Famous Quotation:
"I'm a child of the *civil* rights movement." – Danny Glover, American actor

Related words:
civilized [adjective] Characterized by polite behavior
civilian [noun/person] A citizen who is not in the military service or police department

65.   co·a·li·tion [noun] From Latin *coalitus* ("fellowship")— a group with common interests

Definition: An alliance of people, companies, or countries combined for a common purpose

Usage:

Various groups of women formed a *coalition*, to select a presidential candidate who was the best for women.

The *coalition* of countries formed a common market, to sell their products.

Famous Quotation:

"Any *coalition* has its troubles, as every married man knows." – Arthur Hays Sulzberger, American publisher of the *New York Times*

Related word:

coalesce [verb] To join with others to form a united group

Match the word with the letter of the correct definition.

_____ choose	(a) polite behavior among citizens
_____ chronology	(b) to decide
_____ circulate	(c) the arrangement of when things happen
_____ civil	(d) a group of companies
_____ coalition	(e) to move from place to place

Fill in the blank with the best word. Each word will only be used once.

choose   chronology   circulate   civil   coalition

(a)   Even though Jonathan was angry, he was very _____ to Kim when they met in court.

(b)   To write a summary of the events, it was necessary for Jonathan to have a _____ of when various things happened.

(c)   Jonathan had to _____ a city where he would now live.

(d)   The three countries decided to form a _____ in order to have a common defense against the other nations.

(e)   Aspirin makes the blood thinner, so that it will _____ in the body more rapidly.

66.   co·er·cion [noun] From Latin *coercere* ("to control")— to persuade forcefully

Definition: Being forced to do something

Usage:

The only way to get the people to cooperate was through *coercion*, forcing them to do so.

They agreed that military threats and *coercion* were the only way to get the other countries to join them.

Famous Quotation:

"*Coercion* merely captures man. Freedom captivates him."— Robert McNamara, United States Secretary of Defense

Related word:

coerce [verb] To pressure or threaten someone to do something

67.   co·he·sion [noun] From Latin *cohaesionem* ("sticking together")— sticking together

Definition: The act of binding closely together

Usage:

The team was successful because of their remarkable *cohesion*, sticking together even in times of difficulty.

History creates social *cohesion*, by helping people identify with their past.

Famous Quotation:

"Without social *cohesion*, the human race would not be here." – Peter Gruber, American businessman, educator, and author

Related word:

cohesive [adjective] The characteristic of ticking together

68.   co·in·cide [verb] From Latin *com* ("together") + *incidere* ("to fall upon")—to be in the same place

Definition: To occupy the same place at the same time

Usage:

When your work *coincides* with your idea of fun, it is not work after all.

Their travel schedules *coincide*, because they are going the same direction.

Sometimes everyone's idea of where to go *coincides*, and then there is no argument.

Famous Quotation:

"People are allowed their own opinions, and they don't always *coincide* with yours." – Paul McCartney, British musician

Related words:

coincidence [noun] When two or more things happen at the same time

69.   col·lide [verb] From Latin *com* ("together") + *ladere* ("to strike")— to bump violently

Definition: To come together in a violent impact

Usage:

When a car *collides* with a motorcycle, someone always gets injured.

When political ideas *collide*, the public must vote to decide upon a leader.

Famous Quotation:

"In our ever-changing universe, lives *collide*, and, like runaway planets, we just keep going."— Michael R. French, American author

Related word:

collision [noun] When two things come together violently

70.   com·mod·i·ty [noun] From Latin *commodus* ("convenient")— something convenient to use

Definition: Something useful which can also be sold for profit

Usage:

Toothpaste is a very useful *commodity* which everyone needs.

There is a market for almost every kind of *commodity*, even some that are not needed.

Famous Quotation:

"Gold and silver, like other *commodities*, have an intrinsic value." – David Ricardo, English economist

Match the word with the letter of the correct definition.

_____ coercion   (a) to occupy the same place at once

_____ cohesion   (b) forced to do something

_____ coincide   (c) something useful which can be sold

_____ collide   (d) sticking close together

_____ commodity   (e) to come together with a violent impact

Fill in the blank with the best word. Each word will only be used once.

coercion   cohesion   coincide   collide   commodity

(a)   The company was looking for a new _____ they could sell to teenagers.

(b)   The personalities of Bill and John were different, and were about to _____.

(c)   It would be better if there could be more _____ between them.

(d)   It required much _____ to get Bill and John to agree.

(e)   The manager arranged Bill's travel schedule to _____ with John's.

71.   com·pen·sate [verb] From Latin *com* ("together") + *pendere* ("to weigh")— to offset

Definition: To make a satisfactory payment in return for something

Usage as verb:

He wanted to *compensate* the people who had spent so much time helping him.

She looked for a way to *compensate* the family who had provided her with a place to stay.

Related word:

compensation [noun] The act of paying for something

Usage as noun:

The manager provided the workers with *compensation* for their efforts.

Famous Quotation:

"If we are quiet and ready enough, we shall find *compensation* in every disappointment." – Henry David Thoreau, American author and philosopher

72.   com·plex [adjective] From Latin *com* ("with, together") + *plectere* ("to weave")—with many interwoven parts

Definition: Something with many parts combined together

Usage:

A watch is a *complex* instrument, with a variety of moving parts carefully assembled.

It was a very *complex* story, because they were many different parts woven together.

Famous Quotation:

"I always look at the optimistic side of life, but I am realistic enough to know that life is a *complex* matter." – Walt Disney, American cartoonist and film maker

Related word:

complexity [noun] The condition of something with many parts

73.   com·pli·ca·ted [adjective] From Latin *complicare* ("to fold together")— containing many parts

Definition: Difficult to understand because it has many parts

Usage:

They have a very *complicated* relationship, because they have different desires.

The investigation by the police is *complicated*, because there are so many people involved.

Famous Quotation:

"Life is very simple, but we insist on making it *complicated."* – Confucius, Chinese philosopher

Related word:

complication [noun] Something that is difficult to understand

74.   com·pon·ent [noun] From Latin *com* ("with") + *ponere* ("to put")— an individual part

Definition: One of many parts

Usage:

Each *component* was necessary in order to make the watch work.

The automobile has thousands of *components*, all of which have some purpose.

Famous Quotation:

"True success has more *components* than one sentence or idea can contain." – Zig Ziglar, American author and motivational speaker

75.   com·pro·mise [verb, noun] From Latin *com* ("with, together") + *promittere* ("to promise")— a settlement of differences

Definition: To come to an agreement during a dispute

Usage as a verb:

The two politicians decided to *compromise*, and they agreed to share the stage.

The husband had to *compromise* with his wife about dinner, or else she would not cook it.

Usage as a noun:

The two football teams made a ***compromise***, to take turns using the field.

Famous Quotation:

"A ***compromise*** is the art of dividing a cake in such a way that everyone believes he has the biggest piece." – Ludwig Erhard, Chancellor of Germany

Match the word with the letter of the correct definition.

_____ compensate	(a) to pay someone something
_____ complex	(b) something difficult to understand
_____ complicated	(c) to come to an agreement
_____ component	(d) something which has many parts
_____ compromise	(e) one of many parts

Fill in the blank with the best word. Each word will only be used once.

compensate   complex   complicated   component   compromise

(a)   Purchasing laptops for the students was an important _____ in the school's budget.

(b)   Nate was a good teacher and had worked long hours to help the students succeed, and so it was important to _____ him well for his efforts.

(c)   The course on calculus was very_____ , and difficult to understand.

(d)   The entire building _____ contained a variety of different stores.

(e)   In order to get their votes, the politician had to _____ with some of the people.

76.   con·cen·trate [verb] From Latin *com* ("with") + *centrum* ("center")— to focus on the center

Definition: To think seriously

Usage:

When he realized how many ideas were involved, he had to *concentrate* his thoughts.

Because of the noise in the building, she had to *concentrate* in order to think clearly.

Famous Quotation:

"Do not dwell in the past, and do not dream of the future, but just *concentrate* your mind on the present." – Buddha, Indian sage and philosopher

Related word:

concentration [noun] The act of thinking carefully

77.   con·demn [verb} From Latin *com* ("with") + *damnare* ("to harm")— to 'damn' someone

Definition: To blame someone for doing something wrong

Usage:

She *condemned* him for committing such a crime.

Because of the evidence against him, the jury had no choice except to *condemn* him.

Famous Quotation:

"It is better to risk saving a guilty man than to *condemn* an innocent one." – Voltaire, French philosopher and author

Related word:

condemnation [noun] The act of being blamed for something

78.   con·fi·dence [noun] From Latin *com* ("with") + *fidere* ("to trust")— to have trust

 Definition: To trust someone or something

Usage:

She has *confidence* that her husband will do the right thing for the family.

The manager has **confidence** that his employees will do a good job.

The coach has **confidence** that daily training and exercise will make the team successful.

Famous Quotation:

"If we start without **confidence**, we have already lost half the battle and we bury our own talents." – Pope Francis

Related words:

confident [adjective] Having trust in someone or something

confide [verb] To trust someone and tell them something secret

confidential [adjective] Something secret you only tell people whom you trust

79.   con·flict [noun, verb] From Latin *com* ("together") + *fligere* ("to strike")— to strike

Definition: A fight, or a war

Usage:

The two nations have been in a **conflict** with each other for over ten years.

The world was trying to avoid another military **conflict** in the Middle East.

Famous Quotation:

"Peace is not the absence of **conflict,** but rather the ability to handle **conflict** by peaceful means." – Ronald Reagan, American president

Usage as a verb:

The two ideas **conflict** with each other.

80.   con·quer [verb] From Latin *com* ("with") + *quaerere* ("to gain")— to defeat someone

Definition: To defeat another person or country by force

Usage:

Caesar decided to **conquer** most of the continent of Europe.

Hannibal brought his army and elephants across the Alps in his attempt to **conquer** Rome.

Famous Quotation:

"I believe that anyone can *conquer* fear by doing the things he fears to do." – Eleanor Roosevelt, American humanist and wife of President Franklin D. Roosevelt

Related words:

conquerer [noun/person] Someone who defeats another in war

conquest [noun] The result of having defeated someone in war

Match the word with the letter of the correct definition.

_____ concentrate   (a) to trust a person or thing

_____ condemn   (b) to blame someone

_____ confidence   (c) a fight or war

_____ conflict   (d) to defeat someone or something

_____ conquer   (e) to think about something seriously

Fill in the blank with the best word. Each word will only be used once.

concentrate   condemn   confidence   conflict   conquer·

(a) To take control of Europe, the ancient Romans had to _____ Gaul, which is modern France.

(b) The battle was a major _____ , in a long war.

(c) The Roman government had _____ in Julius Caesar to lead the war.

(d) As part of his military strategy, Julius Caesar decided to _____ on building special bridges to cross the rivers.

(e) When dealing with the enemy, Julius Caesar would often _____ many captured enemy prisoners to death.

Professor Charles Explains Why We Say: *Give them the cold shoulder*

For dinner, houseguests who overstayed their welcome were given the worst part of the animal, not warmed up, the "cold shoulder."

81. con·scious [adjective] From Latin *conscius* ("knowing")— to know what's happening

Definition: Awake and aware

Usage:

She was ***conscious*** of the fact that her dress was torn.

When the boy woke up from the medical operation, he was ***conscious*** again.

Famous Quotation:

"The greatest of faults, I should say, is to be ***conscious*** of none." – Thomas Carlyle, Scottish philosopher and writer

Related words:

consciously [adverb] To be aware of what you are doing

conscience [noun] Your internal measurement of doing something right or wrong

conscientious [adjective] Making an effort to do things right

82. con·se·quence [noun] From Latin *com* ("with") + *sequi* ("to follow")— the result

Definition: The result of having done something

Usage:

Her acceptance into medical school was a direct ***consequence*** of having studied hard in college.

The unfortunate ***consequence*** of playing with fire is that sometimes you can get burned.

Famous Quotation:

"When anger rises, think of the ***consequences***." – Confucius, Chinese philosopher

Related words:

consequently [adverb] As a result of an action

83.   con·sti·tu·tion [noun] From Latin *com* ("with") + *statuere* ("to stand")— rules of where people 'stand' in their relationships to the others in the group.

Definition: A written document describing the laws of a government or some organization

Usage:

The Founders of the United States created a ***Constitution*** which set forth the basic laws of the country.

They women organized their club with a written ***constitution*** of the rules.

Famous Quotation:

"The greatest danger to American freedom is a government that ignores the ***Constitution***." – Thomas Jefferson, American philosopher and president

Related words:

constitutional [adjective] Pertaining to the Constitution

constituency [noun/persons] A group of voters

constituent [noun/person] A voter

84.   con·straint [noun] From Latin *com* ("together") + *stringere* ("to draw tight")— use of force to prevent an action

Definition: The use of pressure, or force, to prevent someone from doing something

Usage:

The police put the prisoner in a ***constraint***, to make sure he caused no harm.

The psychiatrist tried to control the mental patient with a minimum amount of ***constraint***.

The club imposed a ***constraint*** on what the guest speaker could say.

Famous Quotation:

"All ***constraint*** had vanished between the two, and they began to talk."— Edith Wharton, American writer

Related word:

constrain [verb] To use pressure or force to prevent someone from acting

85. con·tam·i·nate [verb] From Latin *com* ('with") + *tangere* ("to touch")—to make impure

Definition: To make unhealthy by touching it with something unclean or unhealthy

Usage:

The water was ***contaminated*** with poison that someone had dumped into it.

The food became ***contaminated*** by the bugs that crawled on it.

After what he did, their relationship was ***contaminated*** by mistrust.

Related words:

contaminant [noun] Something which causes bad health

contamination [noun] The result of touching with something unhealthy

Famous Quotation:

"Cleaning as you go helps keep away **contamination,** and you avoid having food borne bacteria." – Cat Cora, American chef and television personality

Match the word with the letter of the correct definition.

_____ conscious   (a) the written rules of an organization

_____ consequence   (b) to be awake and aware

_____ constitution   (c) to make unclean or unhealthy

_____ constraint   (d) the result of an action

_____ contaminate   (e) using force to prevent something

Fill in the blank with the best word. Each word will only be used once.

conscious   consequence   constitution   constraint   contaminate

(a)   Nate was _____ of the fact that he had a lot of studying to do.

(b)   The rules of the organization were based on its written _____ .

(c)   There was a deadline for completing the course, so Nate was operating under a time _____ to get everything accomplished.

(d)   Nate knew the _____ of not studying was to fail the examination.

(e)   Nate used bottled water, and was careful not to _____ the food with water from the river.

86.   con·tem·plate [verb] From Latin *com* ("with") + *templari* ("to create a space to observe")—to look at carefully

Definition: To think very carefully; to reflect

Usage:

In order to arrive at a good solution, they had to ***contemplate*** for a long time.

The only way to solve the problem is to take time to ***contemplate.***

Famous Quotation:

"Those who ***contemplate*** the beauty of the earth find reserves of strength that will endure as long as life lasts." – Rachel Carson, American marine biologist and conservationist

Related words:

contemplative [adjective] Having the characteristic of thinking hard

contemplation [noun] The act of thinking hard

87.   con·tempt [noun] From Latin *com* ("with") + *temnere* ("to scorn")— scorn or bad feelings

Definition: Seeing something as unworthy or bad

Usage:

 She had ***contempt*** for the man because of his bad behavior.

Everyone has ***contempt*** for someone who harms a child.

Famous Quotation:

"Familiarity breeds ***contempt***." – Aesop, ancient Greek story teller

Related words:

contemptible [adjective] Deserving of bad feelings

contemptuous [adjective] Having bad feelings for someone or something

88.   con·test [noun] From Latin *com* ("together") + *testari* ("to witness")—a game with a witness

Definition: A competition

Usage:

The school held a ***contest*** to see which students would get the best grades.

There was a ***contest*** to see which athletes were the strongest and the fastest.

<u>Famous Quotation</u>:

"Marketing is a ***contest*** for people's attention." – Seth Godin, American author

<u>Related word</u>:

 contestant [noun/person] A participant in a competition

89.   con·text [noun] From Latin *com* ("together") + *texere* ("to weave")— the facts tied together. <u>Definition</u>: The part of a written text that determines what the meaning is. Also, the circumstances in which an event takes place

<u>Usage</u>:

She took his words out of ***context***, and misrepresented what he had said.

It's important to read the entire paragraph, in order to see the ***context*** of what his words mean.

<u>Famous Quotation</u>:

"Power is the chance to impose your will within a certain social ***context***." – Max Weber, German sociologist and philosopher

90.   con·trar·y [adjective] From Latin *contra* ("against")— against something

<u>Definition</u>: Against or opposed

<u>Usage as an adjective</u>:

He always did things which were ***contrary*** to what was expected from him.

Her views were ***contrary*** to the views of the other people in the class.

<u>Famous Quotation</u>:

"The truth is often the exact ***contrary*** of what is generally believed." – Jean de la Bruyere, French philosopher

<u>Related words</u>:

controversy [noun] A disagreement between two or more people

contradictory [adjective] Words or statements which are in disagreement

68

<u>Usage as an adjective:</u>

To say, "The sky is blue" and "The sky is grey" are **contradictory** statements.

Match the word with the letter of the correct definition.

_____ contemplate	(a) a competition between people
_____ contempt	(b) part of a text that determines meaning
_____ contest	(c) to think about very carefully
_____ context	(d) against or opposite
_____ contrary	(e) to have scorn or bad feelings

Fill in the blank with the best word. Each word will only be used once.

contemplate   contempt   contest   context   contrary

(a)   Scott decided to take time and _____ his course of action carefully.

(b)   There will be a difficult _____ to decide who will go to the final competition.

(c)   Many people have _____ for one of the judges.

(d)   It was _____ to the rules of the competition for the participants to say something bad about the judges.

(e)   It was important to understand the _____ of the judge's remarks.

91. con·vey [verb] From Old French *convoier* ("to escort")— to bring to another place
<u>Definition</u>: To take something from one place to another
<u>Usage</u>:
He ***conveyed*** the food from one side of the city to the other side.
Electric wires are used to ***convey*** electricity inside of houses.
He wanted to ***convey*** his best wishes to the new parents.
<u>Famous Quotation</u>:
"You learn … to use your voice to the greatest possible extent possible to ***convey*** emotions."— Helena Bonham Carter, English actress

92. con·vince [verb] From Latin *com* ("together") + *vincere* ("conquer")— to overcome through argument
<u>Definition</u>: To overcome doubts and win the argument
<u>Usage</u>:
The lawyer's responsibility was to ***convince*** the jury that the man was guilty of the crime.
He tried to ***convince*** her that she should marry him.
<u>Famous Quotation</u>:
"It is easier to fool people than to ***convince*** them that they have been fooled." – Mark Twain, American author
<u>Related words</u>:
convict [noun/person] Someone a court decided is guilty of a crime
conviction [noun] The decision that something is true
<u>Usage as a noun</u>:
He was sent to prison because of his **conviction** by the jury at the trial.
In past centuries, it was the **conviction** of many people that the world was flat.

93. core [noun] From Latin *cor* ("heart")—the important center of something
<u>Definition</u>: The heart – or important center – of something
<u>Usage</u>:

The temperature at the *core* of the earth is approximately 5,400 degrees centigrade.

He will never abandon his *core* religious beliefs.

Famous Quotation:

"I admire the fact that the central *core* of Buddhist teaching involves mindfulness and loving kindness and compassion." – Ronald Reagan, American president

94.   coun·ter [adjective, prefix] From Latin *contra* ("against")— against

Definition: Against some person, idea, or country

Usage as adjective:

His approach is *counter* to the usual way of doing things.

She *countered*, that she did not have time to do what he wanted.

Usage as prefix:

The boxer is a *counter*-puncher, because he waits for his opponent to strike first, and then he strikes back.

After the lawsuit was filed against him, he filed a *counter*claim to try to win something himself.

Famous Quotation:

"In the martial arts, whether karate, judo, or Tai Chi, the *counter*attack is the most effective form of self-defense." – Martial Arts instructors

95.   cul·ti·vate [verb] From Latin *cultivare* ("to till, to farm")— to improve and make grow

Definition: To develop and improve

Usage:

The famer had to *cultivate* his soil, so the crops would grow big and healthy.

The company president *cultivated* his relationship with his customers, so that they would buy more of his company's products.

Famous Quotation:

"Observe good faith and justice with all nations. *Cultivate* peace and harmony." – George Washington, first American president

Related words:

cultivation [noun] The process of developing or improving something
cultivated [adjective] Developed or improved

Match the word with the letter of the correct definition.

_____ convey   (a) against
_____ convince   (b) to conquer someone's doubts
_____ core   (c) the center of something
_____ counter   (d) to carry from one place to another
_____ cultivate   (e) to develop and improve

Fill in the blank with the best word. Each word will only be used once.

convey   convince   core   counter   cultivate

(a)   Martha tried to _____ Marc to eat organic food.

(b)   It was difficult for Martha to _____ to Marc how healthy organic food is.

(c)   Martha wanted to get to the _____ of what Marc really believed.

(d)   Whenever she presented an idea, Marc would _____ with an idea of his own.

(e)   To gain Marc's confidence, Martha wanted to _____ a good relationship with him.

96. cur·ric·u·lum [noun] From Modern Latin *curriculum* ("a course")— a course of study

Definition: A course of study at a college

Usage:

To attend medical school, you must study a biology *curriculum* in college.

The students found most of the *curriculum* interesting, but some of it was very difficult.

Famous Quotation:

"I think poetry can help children with the other subjects on the *curriculum* by enabling them to see a subject in a new way." – Carol Ann Duffy, British educator and writer

97. cyn·i·cal [adjective] From Greek *kynos* ("dog-like")— scornful of the motives of others

Definition: Distrust for the motives or integrity of some people

Usage:

She was very *cynical*, and did not believe anything the politician was saying.

The customer was *cynical* about what the salesman was telling her about the quality of the car.

Famous Quotation:

"Inside of every *cynical* person there is a disappointed idealist." – George Carlin, American humorist

Related word:

cynic [noun/person] Someone who does not trust other people

98. De·cem·ber [noun]

Usage:

The month of *December* is when people celebrate Christmas.

Famous Quotation:

"God gave us memory so that we might have roses in *December*." – James M. Barrie, Scottish author

Related words:

decimal [noun] A point in a number system based on ten

decade [noun] A period of ten years

99. de·cline [verb, noun] From Latin *declinare* ("to lower")— to turn down something

Definition: To politely 'turn down' an offer or an invitation

Usage as a verb:

She **declined** his proposal to marry her.

He **declined** an offer to join another company.

Famous Quotation:

"Republics **decline** into democracies, and democracies degenerate into despotisms." – Aristotle, ancient Greek philosopher

Usage as a noun:

The economy of the country is on a **decline**, because business is slowing down.

100. ded·i·cate [verb] From Latin *de* ("away") + *dicare* ("to proclaim as special")—to make separate for a deity or for some religious purpose

Definition: To set apart and regard as special

Usage:

The bishop **dedicated** the new church for the religious congregation.

The priest **dedicated** his life to God.

It was important for the father to **dedicate** his life to the future of his children.

Famous Quotation:

"True strength lies in submission which permits one to **dedicate** his life, through devotion, to something beyond himself." – Henry Miller, American writer

Related word:

dedication [noun] A ceremony in which someone or something is set apart for a special purpose

Professor Charles Explains
Why We Say: *December*

Famous Events in December: *On December 2, 1901 the first trans-Atllantic radio signal was sent by Marconi from England to St. John's Newfoundland with a 500 ft. antenna supported by a kite.*

When there were only 10 months in the old Roman calendar, December was the important 'tenth' (*decem* in Latin) and final month!

_____ curriculum   (a) to go down
_____ cynical   (b) to set apart as special
_____ December   (c) twelfth month of the year
_____ decline   (d) a course of study
_____ dedicate   (e) distrust motives of people

Fill in the blank with the best word. Each word will only be used once.

curriculum   cynical   December   decline   dedicate

(a)   Taylor Swift's birthday is in the month of _____, the same month as Christmas.

(b)   The teachers chose to _____ their lives to helping children learn.

(c)   The teachers spent a long time discussing the _____ for teaching the students.

(d)   Many students _____ to participate in the sports activities of the school.

(e)   The principal of the school was often _____ , when students gave him excuses for not doing their homework.

101. de·duct [verb] From Latin *de* ("away") + *ducere* ("to take")— to remove or take away

Definition: To take away or reduce

Usage:

The cashier *deducted* 10% from the price, because the bread was two days old.

The car dealer would not *deduct* anything from the price.

Famous Quotation:

"We can never *deduct* the unpleasant things we did in our lives, only try to restore them." – Professor Charles

Related word:

deduction [noun]   The amount that was reduced

102. de·grade [verb] From Latin *de* ("down") + *gradus* ("step")— to move down

Definition: To reduce in rank, or to lower in dignity

Usage:

The soldier was *degraded*, from the rank of sergeant to the rank of corporal.

The writer tried to *degrade* the organization, by writing bad newspaper stories about it.

The constant pollution of the air and water *degrades* the planet.

Famous Quotation:

"A union of government and religion tends to destroy government and *degrade* religion." – Hugo Black, American Supreme Court Justice

103. de·i·ty [noun]   From Latin *deus* ("god")— a god

Definition: a god

Usage:

The ancient Greeks had a separate *deity* for love, war, weather, and other things.

Before Christianity, the Sun God was the most popular *deity* in Rome.

Famous Quotation:

"Things we consider mysterious need not be attributed to a *deity*." – Greg Graffin, American musician

Related words:

deify [verb] To consider someone to be a god

104. de·lin·quent [adjective, noun] From Latin *delinquere* ("to fail")— failing to do what is required

Definition: Failing to do what is required; someone who does not obey the law

Usage as an adjective:

He was *delinquent* in paying his rent; so the landlord told him to leave.

The police were looking for young people who were *delinquent* and not attending school.

Usage as a noun:

They were regarded as young *delinquents* because they did not obey the law.

Famous Quotation:

"One good teacher in a lifetime may sometimes change a *delinquent* into a solid citizen." – Phillip Wylie, American author

Related word:

delinquency [noun] The condition of not obeying rules or the law

105. de·mand [verb, noun] From Latin *de* ("completely") + *mandare* ("order")— to ask for urgently

Definition: To insist

Usage as a verb:

The teacher decided to *demand* that the students sit down and stop making noise.

The mother *demanded* that her children study their homework.

Famous Quotation:

"Do your job and *demand* your compensation – but in that order." – Cary Grant, American actor

Usage as a noun:

There was a *demand* for more food by the people who did not have enough to eat.

The people gave the president a list of *demands*.

Match the word with the letter of the correct definition.

_____ deduct   (a) failing to do what is right

_____ degrade   (b) to ask for urgently, or to insist

_____ deity   (c) to take away

_____ delinquent   (d) a god

_____ demand   (e) to reduce in rank

Fill in the blank with the best word. Each word will only be used once.

deduct   degrade   deity   delinquent   demand

(a)   The annual flood of the Nile River in Egypt
_____ some of the villages.

(b)   The Egyptian engineers were _____ in repairing
mud dykes on the river.

(c)   The pharaoh _____ that the farmers repair the
dykes before the October flood.

(d)   The pharaoh told the farmers to _____ the cost of
the repairs from their taxes.

(e)   The favorite _____ of the ancient Egyptians was
Ra, the sun god.

106. de·moc·ra·cy [noun] From Greek *demos* ("the people") + *kratia* ("power")— government by the people

Definition: A government in which the common people have the power.

Usage:

The fundamental purpose of ***democracy*** is to promote the will of the people.

There can never be a pure ***democracy***, since many people won't vote for a variety of reasons.

Famous Quotation:

"The ignorance of one voter in a ***democracy*** impairs the security of all."—John F. Kennedy, American president

Related words:

democrat [noun/person] Someone who believes in the power of the people through voting

democratic [adjective] Believing in government by the people

107. de·mo·graph·ics [noun] From Greek *demos* ("people") + *graphein* ("to write")— the study of characteristics of different human populations

 Definition: The study of characteristics and behavior of people

Usage:

She studied the ***demographics*** of Europe, to understand the European people better.

The marketing man studied the ***demographics*** of the United States, to discover who the best customers were for his products.

Famous Quotation:

"There are a lot of magazines... that only cater to a certain ***demographic*** and only put certain people on their covers." – Zoe Soldana, American actress

Related word:

demography [noun] The study of the human population

108. de·note [verb] From Latin *de* ("completely") + *notare* ("mark out")— to point out
Definition: To indicate or point out
Usage:
A red traffic light ***denotes*** that cars should stop.
When people smile, it usually ***denotes*** that they are happy or pleased with something.
Famous Quotation:
"Though your hair is gray, it does not ***denote*** the age of your heart." – Michael Franklin Ellis, American writer

109. de·ny [verb] From Latin *de* ("away") + *negare* ("to refuse")— to refuse, say 'no'
Definition: To reject a statement or a request
Usage:
The man ***denied*** that he had stolen the property.
The professor ***denied*** the student's request to have more time to study.
Famous Quotation:
"Most men would rather ***deny*** a hard truth, instead of face it." – George R.R. Martin, American writer
Related word:
denial [noun] The act of rejecting something

110. de·scen·dant [noun/person] From Latin *de* ("down") + *scandere* ("climb")— to climb down the ladder of someone's family history
Definition: Someone whose life can be traced to particular parents and grandparents
Usage:
They were part of the British royal family, because they were ***descendents*** of a king.
The religion teacher told the class that everyone is a ***descendent*** of Adam and Eve.

Famous Quotation:

"If you are a good person, the goodness will continue through your *descendants*." – Diane von Furstenberg, Belgian-American fashion designer

Related words:

descend [verb] To come down

descent [noun] The act of coming down

Match the word with the letter of the correct definition.

_____ democracy   (a) to point out

_____ demographics   (b) someone from certain parents

_____ denote   (c) a government by the people

_____ deny   (d) the study of how people act

_____ descendant   (e) to say something is not true

Fill in the blank with the best word. Each word will only be used once.

democracy   demographics   denote   deny   descendant

(a)   Aurora was very proud to have such a famous
_____ in her family's history.

(b)   Aurora _____ that some of her ancestors were also
pirates.

(c)   According to _____ , more men are born than
women.

(d)   Aurora wore her uniform to _____ that she was in
the military.

(e)   The only form of government which allows everyone to vote is a
_____ .

111. des·ig·nate [verb] From Latin *designare* ("to point out")— to point out

Definition: To point to something; to indicate something

Usage:

It was time to ***designate*** the people he wanted on his baseball team.

She had to ***designate*** what dress she wanted.

Famous Quotation:

"The Chinese ***designate*** the wise people by ideographs [signs] for wind and lightning." – Herman Keyserling, German philosopher

Related word:

designation [noun] The act of pointing out

112. de·spise [verb] From Latin *de* ("down") + *specere* ("look")— to look down upon someone or something with scorn.

Definition: To regard someone with contempt

Usage:

The military general ***despised*** any soldiers who refused to fight.

She ***despised*** the idea that women were less qualified than men for the job.

Famous Quotation:

"What do you ***despise***? By this you are truly known." – Michelangelo, Italian artist and sculptor

Related word:

despicable [adjective] Someone or something with bad qualities to be scorned

113. de·spon·dent [adjective] From Latin *despondere* ("to give up")— feeling defeated

Definition: Being sad

Usage:

When her parents died, she was very ***despondent***.

The student was ***despondent***, when he was told that he failed his examinations.

Famous Quotation:

"When health fails, people become *despondent* and even desperate."
– Sri Sathya Sai Baba, Indian guru and philanthropist

114. des·ti·na·tion [noun] From Latin *destinatio* ("place to stand")— the place you are going or directed to go
Definition: The place where you are going
Usage:
They decided that the next *destination* on their trip would be Paris.
His final *destination* was to become a very wealthy man.
Famous Quotation:
"I can't change the direction of the wind, but I can adjust my sails to always reach my *destination*." – James Dean, American actor
Related word:
destiny [noun] The inevitable fate to which someone goes

115. de·tail [noun] From Old French *détail* ("a small piece")— an individual part
Definition: A small part of something
Usage:
He wanted to know every *detail* of how their relationship began.
The newspaper reporter wanted to know the *details* about the life of the scientist.
Famous Quotation:
"It's the little *details* that are vital. Little things make big things happen." – John Wooden, American basketball coach

Match the word with the letter of the correct definition.

_____ designate   (a) the place where you are going

_____ despise   (b) to point

_____ despondent   (c) to look at someone as bad

_____ destination   (d) individual part of something

_____ detail   (e) to be sad

Fill in the blank with the best word. Each word will only be used once.

designate   despise   despondent   destination   detail

(a)   The football team has many miles to go before they reach their

_____ .

(b)   Ron was _____ when he could not drive the van.

(c)   Ron pointed to every _____ on the map.

(d)   The principal _____ the person who would drive the van.

(e)   The driver was someone whom Ron and other students

_____ .

Professor Charles Explains
Why We Say:
Caught Red-Handed

Often people stealing and butchering someone's animals would have blood on their hands . . . and be "*caught red-handed.*"

116. de·tain [verb] From Latin *detinere* ("to hold back")—to keep from proceeding
Definition: To delay, or to prevent someone from proceeding
Usage:
She was *detained*, because the bad weather prevented her from traveling.
The police *detained* the man because they wanted to ask him some questions.
Famous Quotation:
"My thoughts are my company. I can bring them together and *detain* them or dismiss them." – Walter Savage, American writer
Related word:
detainee [noun/person] Someone who has been delayed

117. de·vise [verb] From Old French *deviser* ("to arrange, to plan")—to form a plan
Definition: To create a plan
Usage:
The professor had to *devise* a way to handle the new academic requirements.
The manager had to *devise* a new marketing plan to sell his company's products.
Famous Quotation:
"We should learn from the snail: it has *devised* a home that is both exquisite and functional." – Frank Lloyd Wright, American architect
Related word:
device [noun] Something that is created to make a task easier
Usage as a noun:
The fork is a **device** to make eating easier.

118. dex·ter·ous [adjective] From Latin *dexter* ("on the right" or "right hand")—having 'two right hands'.
Definition: Skillful and adroit, especially with both hands; clever person

The **dexterous** waiter was able to use both hands to remove the dishes from the table.

The mother showed how **dexterous** she could be, by managing three children with only two hands.

Famous Quotation:

"I thank God I was not made a **dexterous** manipulator, because the most important of my discoveries were because of my failures." – Sir Humphrey Davy, English chemist

Related word:

dexterity [noun] Skill and grace in movement

119. di·ag·no·sis [noun] From Greek *dia* ("apart") + *gignoskein* ("to learn")—the act of finding the nature or cause of a disease

Definition: An examination of parts of a body to understand a sickness or disease

Usage:

The doctor made a very careful **diagnosis** of the man's medical problems.

It is important to have a **diagnosis** of the blood, to see what disease the woman has.

Famous Quotation:

"If we can make the correct **diagnosis**, the healing can begin." – Andrew Weil, American physicist and author

Related word:

diagnostic [adjective] Pertaining to the process of examining parts of a body

120. di·lem·ma [noun] From Greek *dilemma* ("double proposition")— two choices at once

Definition: A choice between two options that cannot be combined

Usage:

She has a **dilemma**, to decide either to get married or have a professional career.

The army general had the ***dilemma*** of either waiting for better weather to attack the enemy, or to attack under bad weather conditions.

Famous Quotation:

"The central ***dilemma*** in journalism is that you don't know what it is that you don't know." – Bob Woodward, American journalist and Editor of the *Washington Post*

Match the word with the letter of the correct definition.

_____ detain	(a) to develop a plan to do something
_____ devise	(b) to examine the parts of a body
_____ dexterous	(c) to prevent someone from leaving
_____ diagnosis	(d) a choice between two options
_____ dilemma	(e) skillful with both hands

Fill in the blank with the best word. Each word will only be used once.

detain   devise   dexterous   diagnosis   dilemma

(a)   The medical _____ showed that the Alicia's leg was broken.

(b)   The nurse was amazingly _____ and could use both hands to perform the various things she had to do.

(c)   Alicia's husband had a _____ , either to stay with her at the hospital or go to work.

(d)   Her husband was going to leave, but the doctor decided to _____ him.

(e)   In order to keep Alicia's husband at the hospital, they had to _____ a plan.

121. di·min·ish [verb] From Latin *diminuere* ("break into small pieces")— to reduce
Definition: To make small, or to say that something is not important
Usage:
He tried to ***diminish*** the importance of the situation.
The politician attempted to ***diminish*** the accomplishments of his opponent in the election.
Famous Quotation:
"There are two ways of being happy: we can ***diminish*** our desires or augment our means." – Benjamin Franklin, American inventor and statesman

122. dire [adjective] From Latin *dirus* ("terrible")—having terrible results
Definition: Dreadful or terrible
Usage:
The weatherman warned of ***dire*** consequences from the tornado.
If the disease was not stopped, there would be ***dire*** consequences.
Famous Quotation"
"Nothing has more strength than ***dire*** necessity." – Euripides, Greek philosopher

123. dis·creet [adjective] From Medieval Latin *discretus* ("careful")— prudent, cautious
Definition: Cautious; careful judgment
Usage:
He is very ***discreet***, and he does not want anyone to see him enter the building.
The doctor was ***discreet***, in order not to frighten the family.
Famous Quotation:
"Be ***discreet*** in all things, and so render it unnecessary to be mysterious about any." – Arthur Wellesley, First Duke of Wellington (1759-1852)
Related word:

discretion [noun] The act of being cautious
Usage as a noun:
The leader trusted his assistant and left many decisions to her **discretion**.

124. dis·crim·i·nate [verb] From Latin *discriminare* ("to divide")— to make a clear distinction
Definition: To make a clear distinction between different things or people
Usage:
The designer had to *discriminate*, between dark or light colors for her new dresses.
The manager had to *discriminate*, between educated and uneducated employees.
Related word:
discrimination [noun] The result of making a clear distinction
Famous Quotation:
"In the past, there was active **discrimination** against women in science." – Stephen Hawking, English theoretical physicist and cosmologist

125. dis·ease [noun] From Old French *desaise* ("sickness")— a pathological illness in a part of a body
Definition: A sickness which can go from one person to another
Usage:
The doctor diagnosed the *disease*, and gave his patient the medicine.
The medical authorities tried to stop the *disease* from spreading through the entire city.
Famous Quotation:
"Love is a serious mental *disease*."— Plato, ancient Greek philosopher

Match the word with the letter of the correct definition.

_____ diminish   (a) to make small

_____ dire   (b) cautious; careful judgment

_____ discreet   (c) to make a clear distinction

_____ discriminate   (d) a sickness

_____ disease   (e) terrible

Fill in the blank with the best word. Each word will only be used once.

diminish   dire   discrete   discriminate   disease

(a)   Cancer is a _____ which affects different parts of the body.

(b)   If you do not locate cancer early, the situation could become very _____ .

(c)   The doctor was very _____ when telling the family about their son's cancer.

(d)   Cancer can affect anyone, and it does not _____ between people by gender or race.

(e)   The doctor provided some medicine to _____ the pain.

126. dis·miss [verb] From Latin *dis* ("away") + *mittere* ("send")— to send away

Definition: To send someone away, or to disregard something

Usage:

When the school day was over, the teacher ***dismissed*** all of the students from class.

The professor thought it was a bad idea, and so he ***dismissed*** it from his memory.

Famous Quotation:

"Weak minds usually ***dismiss*** anything which reaches beyond their own understanding." – Francois de La Rochefoucauld, French author

Related word:

dismissal [noun] The act of being sent away

127. dis·re·gard [verb, noun] From Latin *dis* ("apart") + Old French *regardé* ("to look")—to look away

Definition: To look away, or ignore

Usage as a verb:

He ***disregarded*** the impolite comment which the man made to him.

After he lost the election, many people began to ***disregard*** *him*.

Famous Quotation:

"Americans have a penchant for the future and tend to ***disregard*** the past." – Alan Dundes, American educator and folklorist

Usage as a noun:

He has a complete ***disregard*** for the facts.

128. dis·tinct [adjective] From Latin *distinguere* ("keep separate")— separate

Definition: Separate and different

Usage:

The teacher tried to keep his personal beliefs ***distinct*** from what he was teaching his students.

When compared to the clothing of other girls, her clothing was very ***distinct***.

"All things will be clear and ***distinct*** to the man who does not hurry. Haste is blind." – Livy, Roman author

Related word:

distinction [noun] Something which makes a person or thing separate and different.

129. dis·tort [verb] From Latin *dis* ("completely") + *torquere* ("to twist")— to twist

Definition: To twist words or ideas

Usage:

The reporter ***distorted*** what the man had said.

The lawyer knew the only way he could win was to **distort** what the witness said.

Famous Quotation:

"Get the facts first. You can ***distort*** them later."— Mark Twain, American author

Related word:

distortion [noun] The act of twisting words or ideas; something that was twisted

Usage:

What they said was a **distortion** of what she actually told them.

130. di·verse [adjective] From Latin *diversus* ("different ")— different kinds

Definition: Different people or things

Usage:

The country has ***diverse*** ethnic and religious groups.

She read a variety of books, because she had ***diverse*** reading habits.

Related words:

diversify [verb] To create a variety of different things

diversity [noun] A group of different people or things

Famous Quotation:

"If we cannot end our differences, at least we can help make the world safe for **diversity**." – John F. Kennedy, American president

Match the word with the letter of the correct definition.

_____ dismiss	(a) to look the other way
_____ disregard	(b) to twist words or ideas
_____ distinct	(c) to send away
_____ distort	(d) different people or things
_____ diverse	(e) separate

Fill in the blank with the best word. Each word will only be used once.

dismiss   disregard   distinct   distort   diverse

(a)   The teachers were told to _____ the old schedule, and develop a new one.

(b)   According to the new schedule, the teachers were to _____ their classes at 3 PM.

(c)   There was a _____ group of students from many countries in the class.

(d)   One of the students wore a _____ shirt which had many bright colors.

(e)   To get into the class, one of the students tried to _____ his past academic grades.

Why We Say: *Face the Music*

And now - the end is near, and so you face the final curtain..

CARTER

Most say it comes from military firing squads: a blind-folded person stood, back against a wall, unable to see his executioners, but would "*face the music*" (usually drums).

131. do·mes·ti·cate [verb] From Latin *domesticatus* ("to live in a house")— to make someone feel comfortable at home
Definition: To tame an animal, so that it can live with people
Usage:
The man wanted to **domesticate** the lion, and keep it in his house.
Even if you **domesticate** wild animals, some will still be wild if you let them in your house.
Famous Quotation:
"All laws are an attempt to **domesticate** the natural ferocity of our species." – John W. Gardner, American educator
Related word:
domestic [adjective] Referring to something at a home or household
domicile [noun]   A residence or house

132. dy·nam·ic [adjective] From Greek *dynamikos* ("powerful")— full of energy
Definition: Having energy
Usage:
She has a **dynamic** personality, always active.
It was a **dynamic** music performance, with a stage full of singers and dancers.
Famous Quotation:
"Physical fitness is not only one of the most important keys to a healthy body; it is also the basis of **dynamic** and creative intellectual activity." – John F. Kennedy, American president
Related words:
dynamite [noun] An explosive
dynamics [noun] The science of energy forces

133. e·lec·tion [noun] From Latin *ex* ("out of") + *legere* ("to choose")— people choosing a leader
Definition: A voting process, to see who will be the leader
Usage:

There was an *election*, to see who would be president of the United States.

In the local *election* in each city, the voters decide who will be the mayor.

Famous Quotation:

"A politician thinks of the next *election*. A statesman thinks of the next generation." – James Freeman Clarke, American theologian

Related word:

electorate [noun/people]   The people who vote

134. el·e·men·tary [adjective] From Latin *elementem* ("matter in its most basic form") (From the ancient Greeks and Romans, who thought that the four basic *elements* were: earth, air, fire and water.)— the most basic or fundamental part

Definition: Very basic or fundamental

Usage:

Keeping yourself clean in order to stay healthy is *elementary* hygiene.

The little girl was in an *elementary* school, where she would learn the basic knowledge of arithmetic and reading.

Famous Quotation:

"It's *elementary*, Watson." – Sherlock Holmes, a detective in stories of Arthur Conan Doyle, British writer

Related word:

element [noun] Something basic which cannot be reduced

135. e·lite [adjective, noun] From French *élite* ("the best")— special for some reason

Definition: Superior for some reason

Usage as an adjective:

They were *elite* students, because they received A's on their tests.

In order to celebrate their achievements, the *elite* athletes were invited to a party.

Usage as a noun:

The financial *elite* of the country are very wealthy.

Famous Quotation:

"The control of information is something which the *elite* always does, particularly in a despotic form of government." – Tom Clancy, American writer

Related word:

elitism [noun] The belief that some people should be treated better because they are superior in some way

Match the word with the letter of the correct definition.

_____ domesticate	(a) the process of voting
_____ dynamic	(b) basic or fundamental
_____ election	(c) a special group
_____ elementary	(d) to tame an animal
_____ elite	(e) full of energy

Fill in the blank with the best word. Each word will only be used once.

domesticate   dynamic   election   elementary   elite

(a)   The animal trainers in the zoo would try to _____ the animals.

(b)   Heath, the manager of the zoo, is a _____ man with a lot of energy.

(c)   Training the animals was not difficult, because the process is very _____.

(d)   Animal trainers in American zoos are part of an _____ group of educated animal lovers.

(e)   The lion in the zoo became the leader of the animals because of his power, and not by voting in an _____ .

136. em·brace [verb, noun] From Old French *en* ("in") + *brace, braz* ("the arms")— to hold close with your arms

Definition: To hold someone in your arms; to 'hold' something dear to your heart

Usage as a verb:

He *embraced* his wife as soon as he arrived home.

Both parents *embraced* their son, when he returned home from college.

As soon as he heard the new ideas, he *embraced* them.

Famous Quotation:

"To go out with the setting sun on an empty beach is to truly *embrace* your solitude." – Jeanne Moreau, French actress and director

Usage as a noun:

He held her in his *embrace*.

137. e·mis·sion [noun] From Latin *emissionem* ("to send out")— giving out, or sending out matter or energy

Definition: Something sent out

Usage:

The *emissions* from the exhaust of his car were toxic and dangerous.

The *emissions* from the bad wound in his leg were mainly blood and mucous.

Famous Quotation:

"Nuclear power will help provide electricity that our growing economy needs without increasing *emissions*." – Michael Burgess, American politician

Related word:

emit [verb]

Usage as verb:

The car *emitted* exhaust gases from its engine.

138. en·gen·der [verb] From Latin *engendere* ("to give birth")— to create something

Definition: To bring into existence

Usage:

Angry statements often *engender* conflicts or war.

He used his anger to *engender* hostility toward the government.

Famous Quotation:

"It was the experience of mystery... and fear... which *engendered* religion." – Albert Einstein, American scientist

139. en·light·en [verb] From Old English *in* ("on") + *lihtan* (" to shine a light ")— to give intellectual understanding or insight

Definition: To light up an idea; to give intellectual insight

Usage:

By explaining the history of science, the professor attempted to *enlighten* his class.

When the journalist explained things on national television, the entire country was *enlightened*.

Famous Quotation:

"*Enlighten* the people generally, and tyranny and oppression of body and mind will vanish like evil spirits at the dawn of day." – Thomas Jefferson, American president and philosopher

Related word:

Enlightenment [noun] A period of European history that promoted the use of reason to *enlighten* the mind

140. en·ter·pris·ing [adjective] From Old French *entre* ("between") + *prendre* ("to take")— showing a willingness to do something new

 Definition: Showing a willingness and effort to create something

Usage:

He is a very *enterprising* young man, since he always has new ideas.

To raise money for the school, the *enterprising* students sold chocolate candy bars.

Famous Quotation:

"It is the creative and *enterprising* spirit of people that is indispensible. Everything else is supplemental."— Erwin McManus, American author and filmmaker

Related word:

enterprise [noun] An attempt to do something

Match the word with the letter of the correct definition.

_____ embrace   (a) to send out
_____ emission   (b) to provide insight
_____ engender   (c) a willingness to create something
_____ enlighten   (d) to hold
_____ enterprising   (e) to create

Fill in the blank with the best word. Each word will only be used once.

embrace   emission   engender   enlighten   enterprising

(a)   Jack's first job as the new coach was to _____ some cooperation among the athletes on the team.

(b)   After winning any game, the team members would always _____ each other.

(c)   Jack had to _____ the team on a strategy to win games.

(d)   As an _____ coach, Jack created literature to help the training process.

(e)   To avoid the exhaust _____ from the cars, the team did not use the parking lot.

141. en·tre·pre·neur [noun/person] From Old French *entrepredre* ("undertake a challenge")— a person who begins a new venture

Definition: A person who organizes and takes the risk to create something new

Usage:

An ***entrepreneur*** is a person who creates new and exciting companies.

He enjoyed being an ***entrepreneur***, even though it meant working long hours.

Famous Quotation:

"An ***entrepreneur*** assumes the risk, and is dedicated and committed to the success of whatever he or she undertakes." – Victor Kiam, American businessman

Related words:

entrepreneurial [adjective] The spirit of organizing something new

enterprise [noun] A new venture

142. eq·ui·ty [noun] From Latin *aequitas* ("equal")— being fair and just

Definition: The condition of being fair and just; also a financial investment

Usage:

In law, the principal of ***equity*** and fairness was first developed by the ancient Romans.

The judge told the two people that as a matter of ***equity*** they had to share the profits equally.

Buying stock in a company is an investment in the ***equity*** ownership of that company.

Famous Quotation:

"Ethics and ***equity*** and justice do not change with the calendar." – D. H. Lawrence, English author

Related word:

equitable [adjective] Fair and reasonable

143. e·rode [verb] From Latin *ex* ("away) + *rodere* ("gnaw" or "eat")— to wear away

Definition: To wear away slowly

Usage:

Over the centuries the water has ***eroded*** the mountains and created valleys.

If the politician does not keep his promises, the people's trust in him will ***erode***.

Famous Quotation:

"Memories are like stones, because time and distance ***erode*** them like acid." – Ugo Betti, Italian judge and author

Related word:

erosion [noun] The condition of something wearing away

144. er·u·dite [adjective] From Latin *eruditus* ("educated")— extensively educated

Definition: Very educated and scholarly

Usage:

Everyone agreed that the professor was an ***erudite*** man.

The scholar was extremely ***erudite***, but he was unable to have a conversation with an ordinary person.

Famous Quotation:

"An ***erudite*** fool is a greater fool than an ignorant one." – Jean Baptist Moliére, French author

Related word:

erudition [noun] The intellectual quality of knowing many things

145. es·sen·tial [adjective] From Latin *esse* ("to be")— basic and inherent

Definition: The most basic part (the essence)of something

Usage:

Water is an ***essential*** part of human life.

Reading is an ***essential*** part of education.

Famous Quotation:

"The most *essential* part of my day is a proper dinner."— Rachael Ray, American chef and author

Related word:

essence [noun] The most important part of something

Match the word with the letter of the correct definition.

_____ entrepreneur	(a) basic part of something
_____ equity	(b) someone who organizes a new venture
_____ erode	(c) to wear away slowly
_____ erudite	(d) sense of fairness
_____ essential	(e) very educated

Fill in the blank with the best word. Each word will only be used once.

entrepreneur   equity   erode   erudite   essential

(a)   Daniel was an _____ , and was setting up his own research company.

(b)   To get money to build a laboratory, Daniel sold _____ in his new company.

(c)   To do the research, Daniel hired many _____ university professors.

(d)   It was _____ to have confidence in the professors.

(e)   Daniel made sure that nothing would _____ trust in the research.

Professor Charles Explains
Why We Say:
Cut the Red Tape

British solicitors (lawyers) kept their client's documents in a file folder carefully tied with red ribbons. To retrieve papers they would often have to "*cut the red tape*."

146. e·vade [verb] From Latin *evadere* ("escape")— to avoid with cleverness

Definition: To escape through cleverness or deceit

Usage:

By swimming in the river, the escaped convict tried to *evade* the police.

By changing the subject, she tried to *evade* the question.

Famous Quotation:

"We can *evade* reality, but we cannot *evade* the consequences of *evading* reality." – Ayn Rand, Russian-American author

Related word:

evasion [noun] The act of trying to escape

147. ev·i·dence [noun] From Latin *e* ("out of") + *videre* ("to see")— something you can see which makes it easier to decide.

Definition: Visible proof of something

Usage:

The police produced the *evidence* to convict the man of the crime.

To develop a theory, the scientists look at all of the *evidence*.

Famous Quotation:

"A delusion is something that people believe in, despite a total lack of *evidence*." – Richard Dawkins, British biologist and author

Related word:

evident [adjective] To be obvious, once you see it

148. ev·o·lu·tion [noun] From Latin *evolvere* ("to unfold")— a gradual growth process

Definition: A slow process of changing into a more complex form.

Usage:

Through the process of *evolution*, many fish became creatures on land.

Charles Darwin was an English scientist, who wrote about *evolution*.

The *evolution* of science has taken many centuries to reach our present state of knowledge.

Famous Quotation:

"Love is the sacred reserve of energy; it is like the blood of spiritual *evolution*." – Pierre Teihard de Chardin, French paleontologist and author

Related word:

evolve [verb] To develop slowly

Usage as a verb:

During the year, his love for her continually **evolved**.

149. ex·clu·sive [adjective] From Latin *ex* ("out") + *claudere* ("close")— private

Definition: Closed and not shared with others; private

Usage:

It was a very *exclusive* horse club, and only people who owned horses could become members.

He had the *exclusive* legal rights to publish the magazines and sell them.

Famous Quotation:

"Honor is not the *exclusive* property of any political party." – Herbert Hoover, American president

Related word:

exclude [verb] To prevent someone or something from being part of a group

150. ex·ot·ic [adjective] From Greek *exotikos* ("foreign")— from another part of the world

Definition: Intriguing, unusual, or different

Usage:

The lady loved *exotic* plants and flowers from different parts of the world.

The new movie contained many *exotic* costumes from Asia.

Famous Quotation:

"People always like things that seem *exotic*." – Jane Birkin, British music artist

_____ evade	(a) the process of changing slowly
_____ evidence	(b) only open for certain people
_____ evolution	(c) from another part of the world
_____ exclusive	(d) facts to help you decide
_____ exotic	(e) to escape

Fill in the blank with the best word. Each word will only be used once.

evade   evidence   evolution   exclusive   exotic

(a)   Sam was accused of stealing an _____ bird from another country.

(b)   The police had much _____ against Sam for stealing the rare bird.

(c)   When the police asked Sam a question, he tried to _____ it.

(d)   The bird had unusual beauty, created during a long period of _____.

(e)   The man who owned the bird was an _____ dealer in rare animals.

151. ex·pe·di·tious·ly [adverb] From Latin *expedire* (" accomplish quickly")— done with speed and efficiency

Definition: Quickly and efficiently

Usage:

He transferred the cargo from the ships to the trucks as *expeditiously* as possible.

It was necessary for the doctors to provide medical equipment to the hospitals *expeditiously*.

Famous Quotation:

"If people could spread love as *expeditiously* as they spread anger, the world would be more peaceful." – Professor Charles

Related word:

expedite [verb] To speed up the process of getting something done

152. ex·pense [noun] From Latin *expendere* ("weigh out money")— something spent

Definition: The cost to buy something or to accomplish something

Usage:

Buying a new house was a large *expense* for the family.

He worked and became very wealthy, but at the *expense* of his health.

Famous Quotation:

"Earn your success based on service to others, not at the *expense* of others." – H. Jackson Brown, Jr., American writer

Related word:

expensive [adjective] Something that costs a lot

153. ex·pe·ri·ence [noun, verb] From Latin *ex* ("out of") + *experiri* ("to test")— learning something through the senses

Definition: Learning something personally – by feeling it or seeing it

Usage as a noun:

She had the wonderful *experience* of meeting the famous singer personally at the concert.

Taking an ocean voyage was an *experience* they would never forget.

Famous Quotation:

"You cannot create *experience*. You must undergo it."—Albert Camus, French journalist and author

Usage as a verb:

He had to personally *experience* the joy of skydiving, before he knew how much fun it is.

Related word:

experiment [verb] To test something in order to learn from it

154. ex·ploit [verb, noun] From Old French *esploit* ("gain advantage")— an act or deed

Definition: To use something to your advantage; an heroic deed

Usage as a verb:

The Polynesians *exploit* the natural resources of the ocean, whether it is sailing, swimming, or fishing.

The politician *exploited* every opportunity to become more popular with the public.

Famous Quotation:

"Any fool can have bad luck; the art consists in knowing how to *exploit* it." – Frank Wedekind , German playwright

Usage as a noun:

Lawrence of Arabia wrote a book about his exciting *exploits* called *Seven Pillars of Wisdom*.

Related word:

exploitation [noun] The process of using something to your advantage

155. ex·tend [verb] From Latin *ex* ("out") + *tendere* ("to stretch")— to lengthen

Definition: To make longer or stretch out

Usage:

The electrician *extended* the length of the television antenna by pulling it out further.

To complete his studies, the student had to *extend* his time at school.

He wanted to *extend* the relationship with her, but she wanted to end it.

Famous Quotation:

"People who live long have one or two lines which **extend** across their entire hand." – Aristotle, ancient Greek philosopher

Related word:

extension [noun] Something which is made longer

Match the word with the letter of the correct definition.

_____ expeditiously   (a) learning by seeing, touching or thinking

_____ expense   (b) quickly

_____ experience   (c) to use to your advantage

_____ exploit   (d) to make longer

_____ extend   (e)the cost

Fill in the blank with the best word. Each word will only be used once.

expeditiously   expense   experience   exploit   extend

(a)   Paying the cost of a two week vacation to Europe was a big
_____ .

(b)   Both parents knew the trip would be a wonderful
_____ for their children.

(c)   In preparing for the trip, the parents acted as
_____ as possible.

(d)   To make the trip longer, they decided to _____ it by
one week.

(e)   They wanted to have more time to _____ the
opportunities in various countries.

156. ex·tin·guish [verb] From Latin *ex* ("out") + *stinguere* ("quench")— to quench; to end
Definition: To put an end to something
Usage:
The firemen brought in water, to ***extinguish*** the fire.
He paid the money, in order to ***extinguish*** the debt.
The dinosaurs were ***extinguished*** by an asteroid, which hit the earth over 66,000,000 years ago.
Famous Quotation:
"A good reputation is like fire. If you ***extinguish*** it, you will not easily kindle it again." – Francis Bacon, English philosopher and statesman
Related word:
extinction [noun] The result of something which is no longer in existence
extinct [adjective] To no longer be in existence
Usage:
The dinosaurs are **extinct**, except some of their descendants, for example birds.

157. ex·tract [verb, noun] From Latin *ex* ("out") + *trahere* ("to draw")— to remove
Definition: (As a verb): to take something out of the ground, or out of a document; (as a noun), something which is removed
Usage as a verb:
The miner tried to ***extract*** all of the gold from the ground.
The dentist decided to ***extract*** the bad tooth from his patient.
The writer wanted to ***extract*** the most important words from the poem.
Famous Quotation:
"The only lesson to ***extract*** from civil war is that it is pointless, futile and ugly." – Anthony Minghella, British director and filmmaker
Usage as a noun:
The ***extract*** which the scientist obtained from the chemical was a small amount of iron.
Related word:

extraction [noun] The process of removing something

158. ex·treme [adjective, noun] From Latin *extremus* ("outside") – remote in any way

Definition: Outside of the normal or usual

Usage as an adjective:

The weather had reached a temperature of ***extreme*** heat.

To pay for the many government programs, the politician favored ***extreme*** taxation.

Famous Quotation:

"Writing is an ***extreme*** privilege, but it is also a gift. It's a gift to yourself, and a gift of giving a story to someone." – Amy Tan, American writer

Usage as a noun:

His political views went from one ***extreme*** to another.

Related word:

extremely [adverb] Out of the ordinary

Usage as an adverb:

It's **extremely** cold outside.

159. false (adjective) From Latin *fallere* ("to deceive" or "to lie")— not true.

Definition: Not true; contrary to facts

Usage:

He provided the police with a ***false*** statement of where he was when the crime occurred.

The explanation the little girl told her mother was ***false***.

Famous Quotation:

"To thine own self be true, and it must follow as the night the day, thou canst not then be ***false*** to any man." – William Shakespeare, English author and playwright

Related words:

falsehood [noun] Something which is not true; a lie.

falsify [verb] To make something no longer true

Usage as verb:

He **falsified** the documents by changing the names on them.

160. fa·mil·iar [adjective] From Latin *familiaris* ("family")— seen or heard often
Definition: Seen or heard often; well known
Usage:
She was very *familiar* with him, since she had often seen him in class.
It was a *familiar* fairy tale, which people had been telling their children for many years.
Famous Quotation:
"The simplest schoolboy is now *familiar* with truths for which Archimedes would have sacrificed his life."— Ernest Renan, French author
Related word:
familiarity [noun] The condition of being well known to someone

Match the word with the letter of the correct definition.

_____ extinguish   (a) to take out

_____ extract   (b) out of the ordinary

_____ extreme   (c) to put an end to something

_____ false   (d) well known

_____ familiar   (e) not true

Fill in the blank with the best word. Each word will only be used once.

extinguish   extract   extreme   false   familiar

(a)   Because Mary knew the people, the faces in the photo looked
_____ to her.

(b)   To save one of the photos, Mary tried to _____ it
from the fire.

(c)   The _____ heat of the fire made it difficult to
remove the photo.

(d)   Mary's little brother tried to _____ the fire.

(e)   Mary's little brother gave a _____ explanation of
how the fire started.

161. fam·ine [noun] From Latin *fames* ("hunger")— drastic food shortage

Definition: A wide-spread food shortage affecting many people

Usage:

During the Irish *famine* in the 19th century, millions of people died.

The United States donates tons of food to people affected by *famines*.

Famous Quotation:

"Years of drought and *famine* come, and years of flood and *famine* come, and the climate is not changed with chance, libation, or prayer."— John Wesley Powell, American geologist and author

Related word:

famished [adjective] Very hungry

162. fa·tal [adjective] From Latin *fatalus* ("ordered by fate")— causing death

Definition: Causing death

Usage:

The automobile accident was *fatal* for everyone in the car.

For hundreds of people in the city, the spread of the disease became *fatal*.

The military officer made the *fatal* decision to send in more troops.

Famous Quotation:

"Success is not final, and failure is not *fatal*. It is the courage to continue that counts." – Winston Churchill, British Prime Minister and author

Related word:

fatality [noun] A death

163. fea·si·ble [adjective] From Latin *facere* ("to make")— able to be done

Definition: Capable of being done

Usage:

The builder told his customer that it was *feasible* to build the house before winter.

The coach knew that it was *feasible* for his football team to win the tournament.

<u>Famous Quotation</u>:

"Divide each difficulty into as many parts as is *feasible* and necessary to resolve it." – Rene Descartes, French mathematician and philosopher

<u>Related word</u>:

feasibility [noun] Something which can be accomplished

164. fea·ture [noun, verb] From Latin *factura* ("a formation")— part of an appearance

<u>Definition</u>:   A part of some formation, like the nose, eyes and mouth are part of the face; also, to become some important part of an event

<u>Usage as a noun</u>:

Her beautiful eyes were the best *feature* on her face.

His sense of humor was a charming *feature* of his personality.

<u>Famous Quotation</u>:

"I just believe that our most redeeming *feature* as a species is our capacity for love." – Amanda McBroom, American singer and musician

<u>Usage as a verb</u>:

The movie *featured* three very famous actors.

165. Feb·ru·ar·y [noun]

<u>Usage</u>:

On *February* 2, 1848, the U.S. and Mexico signed the Treaty of Guadalupe Hidalgo to end the war, and the U.S. paid Mexico $15,000,000 for parts or all of various areas of California, Arizona, New Mexico, Texas, Nevada, Utah, Colorado, and Wyoming.

On *February* 3, 1870 the 15th Amendment to the U.S. Constitution was ratified, guaranteeing the right of citizens to vote regardless of race, color, or previous servitude.

<u>Famous Quotation</u>:

 "Thirty days hath *September*… April, June and November; *February* has twenty-eight alone, and all the rest have thirty-one; except in Leap Year, that's the time, when *February's* days are twenty-nine."

Match the word with the letter of the correct definition.

_____ famine	(a) causing death
_____ fatal	(b) able to be done
_____ feasible	(c) a food shortage
_____ feature	(d) second month of the year
_____ February	(e) a part of something or someone

Fill in the blank with the best word. Each word will only be used once.

famine   fatal   feasible   feature   February

(a)   When there is no rain, it is not _____ to grow potatoes.

(b)   Over one million people died in the Irish potato _____ in the 19th century.

(c)   For those with no food, the hunger was _____ .

(d)   Starvation was the most common _____ of the situation.

(e)   The cold weather in _____ made conditions even worse.

Professor Charles Explains
Why We Say: *February*

The ancient Roman festival of "purification" (*Februalia*) was the month of spring cleaning and moral cleansing, later personified by the Roman god *Februus*.

166. fer·til·ize [verb] From Latin *feretilis* ("productive")— to help something grow

Definition: To help something to grow

Usage:

To have a good crop of corn this year, the farmer had to *fertilize* the soil

To create a baby, the sperm must *fertilize* the ovum.

Famous Quotation:

"Life should be a struggle of desires toward adventures whose nobility will *fertilize* the soul." – Rebecca West, British author

Related words:

fertilizer [noun] Something used to help things grow

fertile [adjective] Something spread on the soil to help plants grow

Usage as an adjective:

The soil was **fertile**, and so it was easy for crops to grow.

167. flood [noun, verb] From Old English *flod* ("flowing water")— an overflow of something

Definition: An overflow of something.

Usage as a noun:

The *flood* from the river water ruined all of the farmer's crops.

When the reservoir broke, the *flood* of water destroyed many of the houses in the town.

She was so upset, that she cried a *flood* of tears.

Famous Quotation:

"The *flood* of money that gushes into politics today is a pollution of democracy." – Theodore White, American writer

Usage as a verb:

The professor decided to *flood* his students with facts.

168. fluc·tu·ate [verb] From Latin *fluctuare* ("to move in waves")— to move in waves

Definition: To vary irregularly, up and down

Usage:

The price of the stocks on the world stock markets *fluctuate* every day.

He was either happy or sad, since his mood would **fluctuate** with how much money he made or lost.

Famous Quotation:

"It's easier to stay in shape than to **fluctuate**." — Lou Diamond Phillips, American actor

Related word:

fluctuation [noun] The condition of going up and down

169. flour·ish [verb] From Latin *florere* ("to blossom")— to thrive

Definition: To grow well and thrive

Usage:

The flowers in her garden **flourished**, because of so much rain and sun.

Once he completed his education, his career **flourished**.

Famous Quotation:

"Studies show that children best **flourish** when one mom and one dad are there to raise them." – John Boehner, American politician, Speaker of the House of Representatives

170. fo·cus [verb, noun] From Latin *focus* ("fireplace")— where the family met

Definition: A center of interest or importance

Usage as a verb:

In order to pass their examinations, the students had to **focus** on their studies.

Instead of going to the movies, she decided to **focus** on her artwork.

Famous Quotation:

"I find hope in the darkest days, and **focus** in the brightest. I do not judge the universe."— Dalai Lama, religious leader of Tibetan Buddhism

Usage as a noun:

The broken bone in the man's leg was the **focus** of the doctor's attention.

Related word:

focal point [noun] The spot on which people concentrate their eyes or thoughts

Match the word with the letter of the correct definition.

_____ fertilize   (a) to go up and down

_____ flood   (b) to help grow

_____ fluctuate   (c) to grow well and thrive

_____ flourish   (d) a point where things meet

_____ focus   (e) an overflow of something

Fill in the blank with the best word. Each word will only be used once.

fertilize   flood   fluctuate   flourish   focus

(a)   The water from the _____ destroyed much of the farm.

(b)   The farmer had to _____ on removing the water from the fields.

(c)   Then the farmer had to _____ the fields, in order to help the crops grow.

(d)   When the sun came out, the new crops began to _____.

(e)   The mood of the farmer would _____ with the weather.

171. foil [verb, noun] From Old French *foler* ("to trample on")— to prevent

Definition: (verb) To prevent from being successful; (noun) a fencing sword

Usage as a verb:

The police *foiled* the attempt by the robbers to rob the bank.

Usage as a noun:

When the two men were fencing, they used their fencing *foils* to strike each other.

Famous Quotation:

"I'm a convenient *foil* for a lot of people." – Kevin Costner, American actor and director

172. folk·lore [noun] From Old English *folc* ("common people") + *lar* ("learning")— ancient beliefs of common people

Definition: Traditional beliefs or myths of a group of people, passed down orally

Usage:

She believed everything about the *folklore* of her people, including dragons.

He regarded *folklore* as superstitions for ignorant people.

Famous Quotation:

"When fairy tales are written in the West, they are known as *folklore*. In the East, fairy tales are
called 'religions'." – Paul Henderson, British author

173. fore·cast [verb, noun] From Latin *fore* ("before") + *casten* ("prepare")— to predict

Definition: To estimate and predict in advance

Usage as a verb:

Based upon their survey of the people, the polling company *forecast* the results of the election.

The weatherman *forecast* the temperature of the weather for the entire week.

Famous Quotation:

"The most reliable way to ***forecast*** the future is to try to understand the present." – John Naisbitt, American author

Usage as a noun:

The weather ***forecast*** was for more rain.

174. fo·ren·sics [noun] From Latin *forensis* ("forum"—for a court)—concerning words for public discussion

Definition: The study of the rules of debate; something used for a court of law

Usage:

She studied ***forensics***, in order to understand the rules of formal debate.

The lawyer used his knowledge of ***forensics*** to present his arguments in court.

Related words:

forensic science/forensic medicine   Branches of science that establish facts about human behavior

Famous Quotation:

"Going back to the British detective, Sherlock Holmes, we have a tradition of **forensic science** in detective stories."— Jeffery Deaver, American mystery writer

175. for·mal [adjective] From Latin *formare* ("to shape")— the outward appearance

Definition: The outward form or structure of something

Usage:

He had a ***formal*** education, since he attended the regular schools.

She gave the ***formal*** greeting to the king, which meant she had to bow.

Famous Quotation:

"It's a miracle that curiosity survives ***formal*** education." – Albert Einstein, American scientist

Related word:

formality [noun] The quality of being formal

Match the word with the letter of the correct definition.

_____ foil	(a) to predict
_____ folklore	(b) the rules of debate
_____ forecast	(c) the outward form or appearance
_____ forensics	(d) to prevent someone or something
_____ formal	(e) traditional myths or beliefs

Fill in the blank with the best word. Each word will only be used once.

foil   folklore   forecast   forensics   formal

(a)   The college had an exhibition about the history and _____ of the early Americans.

(b)   The professors used the science of _____ to determine the age of the historical items.

(c)   Since it was a _____ event, Jeffrey dressed well.

(d)   The weather _____ was for sunshine the entire day.

(e)   Installing cameras helped to _____ any attempt by people to touch the exhibits.

176. for·ti·fy [verb] From Old Latin *fortificare* ("to strengthen")—to make stronger

Definition: To make strong

Usage:

The king decided to *fortify* the castle against his enemies.

He *fortified* his body, by eating healthy food.

By obtaining more facts to support his ideas, the scientist *fortified* his theory.

Famous Quotation:

"*Fortify* yourself with contentment, for it is an impregnable fortress." – Epictetus, ancient Greek philosopher

Related word:

fort, fortification [nouns] Strong structures built as a defense

177. foun·da·tion [noun] From Latin *fundus* ("the bottom")— the base on which something stands

Definition: The base of a building, or of an organization, or of an idea

Usage:

To secure the building, the builder laid the *foundation* for the building 10 feet deep.

They created the *foundation* for the organization, by developing a set of rules.

Her college degree became the *foundation* for her future success in science.

Famous Quotation:

"A successful man is one who can lay a firm *foundation* with the bricks which others have thrown

at him." – David Brinkley, American journalist

Related word:

founder [noun/person] Someone who creates something from the beginning

178. fre·quent [adjective] From Latin *frequentia* ("assembly in great numbers")— often

Definition: Occurring often

Usage:

She was a *frequent* visitor to the library.

He made *frequent* visits to his sick relatives, in order to make them feel better.

Related words:

frequency [noun] Describing the number of times something occurs

frequently [adverb] Happening often

Famous Quotation:

"Sometimes it's more important how well you do something, rather than how **frequently** you do it." – Professor Charles

179. func·tion [noun, verb] From Latin *functionem* ("performance")— the purpose

Definition: The purpose for which something is designed

Usage as a noun:

It is the *function* of the air conditioner to bring cool air into the building.

They were going to a fund-raising *function*, in order to raise money for charity.

Famous Quotation:

"Criticism may not be agreeable, but it is necessary. It fulfills the same *function* as pain in the body. It calls attention to an unhealthy state of things." – Winston Churchill, British Prime Minister and author

Usage as a verb:

Because one wheel is broken, the bicycle does not *function* well.

Related word:

functional [adjective] Something that works properly

180. fur·nish [verb] From Old French *furniss* ("to provide")— to give what is needed

Definition: To provide what is needed

Usage:

She *furnished* her new home with modern furniture.

For their examination, the teacher decided to *furnish* the class with some paper.

The woman *furnished* the writer with some ideas for his book.

Famous Quotation:

"It is the food which you *furnish* to your mind that determines the whole character of your life." – Emmet Fox, Irish author

Related word:

furnishings/furniture [nouns] Things you put in your home or office to make them comfortable

Match the word with the letter of the correct definition.

_____ fortify	(a) occurring often	
_____ foundation	(b) to make strong	
_____ frequent	(c) the action for which something is made	
_____ function	(d) to provide what is needed	
_____ furnish	(e) the bottom of something	

Fill in the blank with the best word. Each word will only be used once.

fortify   foundation   frequent   function   furnish

(a)   The Eskimo in Alaska built his home with a strong _____ to support high walls.

(b)   To protect himself from the strong winds, the Eskimo had to _____ the walls with seal hides.

(c)   The seal hides also had the _____ of keeping heat inside of the home.

(d)   He expected to have _____ visitors to his new home.

(e)   To make it nice, he had to _____ his home with bear rugs for people to sit.

181. fu·tile [adjective] From Latin *futilis* ("worthless")— having no useful result

Definition: Having no useful result

Usage:

The entire voyage was *futile*, since they did not make any new discoveries.

Searching for gold in those mountains was a *futile* endeavor.

Because the public did not like his ideas, his entire election campaign was a *futile* effort.

Famous Quotation:

"Basing our happiness on our ability to control everything is *futile*." – Stephen R. Covey, American educator and author

Related word:

futility [noun] Something which is a waste of time

182. gain [verb] From Old French *gaaigne* ("to acquire")— to get something

Definition: To obtain something, usually by your effort

Usage:

He wanted to *gain* weight, in order to be on the football team.

She tried to *gain* a good reputation as a designer of fancy dresses.

Famous Quotation:

"The easiest way to *gain* someone's trust is to deserve it." – Ashly Lorenzana, American writer

183. ga·la [noun] From Old French *galer* ("to make merry")— a big party

Definition: A festive social event

Usage:

She purchased a new dress for the big *gala* next Saturday.

He wanted to drive his new limousine to the *gala* at the villa.

Famous Quotation:

"It's an honor to share this Annual Awards *Gala* with so many like-minded individuals who want nothing more than to make this world a better place." – William Austin, English actor

Related word:

gallant [adjective] The attire and behavior of a man of fashion

184. gale [noun] From Old Norse *gol* ("breeze")— a strong wind of 32 to 63 miles per hour

Definition: A very strong wind

Usage:

The ships were caught in a *gale* in the ocean.

There was a *gale* of criticism against the politician, because of what he did.

Famous Quotation:

"Let the winds blow! A fiercer *gale* is wild within me?" – Edmund Clarence Stedman, American poet and author

185. gap [noun] From Old Norse *gap* ("space")— a space in a wall

Definition: An opening in a solid surface

Usage:

There is a major *gap* in the castle wall, allowing the enemy soldiers to enter.

He recognized that there was a *gap* in his argument, and he was going to lose.

Famous Quotation:

"Your problem is to bridge the *gap* between where you are now and the goal you intend to reach." – Earl Nightingale, American motivational speaker and author

_____ futile	(a) a strong wind
_____ gain	(b) having no useful result
_____ gala	(c) an opening
_____ gale	(d) to get or acquire
_____ gap	(e) a festive event

Fill in the blank with the best word. Each word will only be used once.

futile   gain   gala   gale   gap

(a)   Nate worked hard and hoped he would _____ a fortune from his efforts.

(b)   To promote his new company, Nate planned to have a _____ and invite important people.

(c)   Nate knew it would be _____ to try to keep his competitors away from the event.

(d)   The night of the event they expected a big storm, probably a _____.

(e)   One of Nate's workers could not come, so his brother said he would fill the _____.

186. gen·der [noun] From Greek *genos* ("species")— sexual identity

Definition: Sexual identity (male or female)

Usage:

The lioness was born of the female *gender*.

When they apply for certain jobs, women often face *gender* discrimination.

Famous Quotation:

"I'm not limited by my *gender*, and I don't think anyone else should be either." – Ellen Barkin, American actress and film producer

187. gen·er·a·tion [noun] From Latin *genus* ("to give birth")— offspring from an ancestor

Definition: The offspring of a common ancestor, from the same time period of descent

Usage:

His grandfather's *generation* was involved in World War II.

The next *generation* will have even more technology than we have.

Famous Quotation:

"The philosophy of the school room in one *generation* will be the philosophy of the government in
the next." – Abraham Lincoln, American president

188. gen·u·ine [adjective] From Latin *genuinus*, from *genu* ("the knee")... (From the Roman custom of a father placing a newborn on his knee to acknowledge paternity.)— legitimate

Definition: Real, true, or legitimate.

Usage:

It was a *genuine* misunderstanding, not simply some act.

Her feelings for him are *genuine*, because she really loves him.

Famous Quotation:

"The true secret of happiness lies in taking a *genuine* interest in all of the details of daily life." – William Morris, English author

189. ge·ol·o·gy [noun] It is the science of studying the earth's crust, from Greek *geo* ("earth") + *logia* ("study").

Usage:

His study of *geology* taught him the age of the planet earth.

One way to study *geology* is to study earthquakes.

Famous Quotation:

"*Geology* holds the keys to one of the kingdoms of nature..." – William Buckland, English geologist and theologian

Related words:

petrology [noun] From Greek *petros* (rock) + *logia* (study), the study of rocks,

anthropology [noun] From Greek *anthropos* (mankind) + *logia* (study), the study of mankind

190. gov·ern [verb] From Latin *gubernare* "(to rule")— to rule

Definition: To exercise authority over other people

Usage:

The president was elected by the people to *govern* the nation.

The dictator used his army and police force to *govern* the people in his country.

Famous Quotation:

"No man is good enough to *govern* another man without the other's consent." – Abraham Lincoln, American president

Related word:

government [noun] The people who have the authority to manage

It is the science of studying the earth's crust. From Greek *geo* ("earth") + *logia* ("discourse" or "study"). It's similiar to petrology, the study of rocks, Greek *petros* + *logia*.

Match the word with the letter of the correct definition.

_____ gender   (a) real or true

_____ generation   (b) sexual identity

_____ genuine   (c) the study of the earth

_____ geology   (d) to exercise authority

_____ govern   (e) offspring at same stage of descent

Fill in the blank with the best word. Each word will only be used once.

gender   generation   genuine   geology   govern

(a)   Every young _____ in history has a new set of ideas for the world.

(b)   Taylor decided to study science, loved being outside, and wanted to learn _____.

(c)   Because of her female _____, Taylor's father told her it might be difficult for her.

(d)   However, Taylor had a _____ interest in learning as much as she could.

(e)   Her father told her that sometimes it was easier to _____ a nation than to _____ one's own desires.

191. grat·i·tude [noun] From Latin *gratus* ("thankful")—
thankfulness

Definition: Being thankful

Usage:

She expressed her ***gratitude*** to her teachers, for the help they had given her.

He wanted to show his ***gratitude*** to his parents, for everything they had done for him.

Famous Quotation:

"When we express our ***gratitude***, we must never forget that the highest appreciation is not to utter words, but to live by them." – John F. Kennedy, American president

Related word:

grateful [adjective] Feeling thankful

192. gro·tesque [adjective] From Italian *grottesco* ("of a cave")—
distorted appearance

Definition: Ugly or distorted appearance

Usage:

It was a ***grotesque*** painting, with many distorted creatures in it.

When the witch looked into the mirror, she saw a ***grotesque*** image of an ugly woman.

Famous Quotation:

"Oh sleep! – a ridiculous mystery which makes faces appear so ***grotesque***." – Guy de Maupassant, French author

193. guilt [noun] From Old English *gylt* ("failure of moral duty")—
responsible for doing something wrong

Definition: Being responsible for doing something wrong

Usage:

The man admitted his ***guilt*** for stealing the money.

When she was questioned, she admitted her ***guilt***.

Famous Quotation:

"Alas! How difficult it is not to betray one's *guilt* by one's looks." – Ovid, ancient Greek thinker

Related word:

guilty [adjective] How someone is regarded when they have something wrong

Usage as an adjective:

After looking at the evidence, the judge found the man **guilty** of committing the crime.

194. gut [noun, verb] From Old English *guttas* ("a channel" -- inside of the stomach)—the intestine or stomach

Definition: (noun) The alimentary canal in the intestine; (verb) to remove the inner organs

Usage as a noun:

The *gut* is an essential part of the stomach, and it processes the food when we eat.

He told the class that sometimes he trusts his *gut*, and can sense something is right or wrong.

Famous Quotation:

"Experience has taught me a few things. One is to listen to your *gut*, no matter how good something sounds on paper." – Donald Trump, American businessman and politician

Usage as a verb:

The butcher had to *gut* the deer, before he could cut it up into slices of meat.

The editor decided to *gut* the young writer's book, and he removed most of the text.

Related word:

guts [noun] An expression of courage.

Usage as an expression:

The man had a lot of **guts** because of the brave thing he did.

195. hab·it·a·ble [adjective] From Latin *habitabilis* ("fit for living")— suitable for living

Definition: A place suitable for you to live

They looked around the town for days, before they found a house that was *habitable*.

They had to build a shelter which was *habitable* for the cold weather.

Related word:

inhabitant [noun/person] Someone who lives in a particular location

Famous Quotation:

"Every **inhabitant** of this planet must contemplate the day when this planet may no longer be *habitable*." – John F. Kennedy, American president

Related words:

habitation, **habitat** [nouns] Natural places for people or animals to live

Match the word with the letter of the correct definition.

_____ gratitude   (a) ugly

_____ grotesque   (b) part of the stomach

_____ guilt   (c) being thankful

_____ gut   (d) suitable for living

_____ habitable   (e) responsible for doing something wrong

Fill in the blank with the best word. Each word will only be used once.

gratitude   grotesque   guilty   gut   habitable

(a)   Bob, the architect, designed an ugly building which looked

_____ .

(b)   The building was so poorly built that it was not even

_____.

(c)   When everyone told Bob how bad the building was, Bob began to feel _____ .

(d)   Bob felt so bad, he felt someone had hit him in the

_____ .

(e)   Bob said he was sorry, but no one expressed any
_____ for his apology.

196. hag·gle [verb] From Old High German *hacchon* ("to cut")— to bargain on a price

Definition: To bargain, and try to reduce the price

Usage:

If you want to get a lower price, sometimes you have to **haggle** with the salesman.

It was difficult for her to **haggle** about money.

Famous Quotation:

"After all my years in baseball, there are two things I've never gotten use to – **haggling** with a player over his contract, and telling a boy he has to go back." – Connie Mack, American baseball player and manager

197. hal·lu·ci·nate [verb] From Latin *alucinatus, hallucinatus* ("wander in the mind")— 'seeing' things which are not there

Definition: Seeing things that are not there: from a mental disorder or a reaction to drugs or alcohol; a false sense of reality

Usage as a verb:

He **hallucinated** so much, that people stopped believing what he said.

The woman had hit her head on a rock, and so she would often **hallucinate**.

Whenever the man had too much alcohol to drink, he would **hallucinate**.

Related words:

hallucinatory [adjective]   Characterized by imagining

hallucinogen [noun] A substance or drug that induces false images

hallucination [noun] The act of seeing things which are not there

Usage as a noun:

Where is the border between having a vivid imagination, and having **hallucinations**?

Famous Quotation:

"Imagination comes to an open mind, but what comes to an empty mind is just a **hallucination**." – Anjuj Somany, Indian writer

198. ha·rass [verb] From French *harasser* ("to annoy") possibly from Old French *harer* ("to set a dog on")— to annoy or irritate
Definition: To annoy or constantly torment
Usage:
The boy was always trying to **harass** his little sister.
The children **harassed** their mother, until she finally let them go outside to play.
Famous Quotation:
"I've been chased by paparazzi (photographers)... and they chase you and **harass** you the whole time." – Tom Cruise, American actor
Related word:
harassment [noun] Annoying someone

199. haz·ard·ous [adjective] From Middle French *hasardeux* ("perilous")— dangerous
Definition: Dangerous
Usage:
Hannibal and his elephants made a **hazardous** journey over the mountains in winter time.
The freezing temperatures and the ice made Robert Peary's trip to the Arctic very **hazardous**.
Famous Quotation:
"We think of first love as sweet and valuable— a blessed if **hazardous** condition." – Roger Ebert, American movie critic
Related word:
hazard [noun] A source of danger

200. he·don·is·tic [adjective] From Greek *hedone* ("pleasure")— devoted to pleasure
Definition: Devoted to pleasure
Usage:
He was entirely **hedonistic**, always drinking and partying.
Many ancient Romans were involved in **hedonistic** behavior.
Related words:

hedonism [noun] The condition of loving only pleasure
hedonist [noun/person] Someone who only loves pleasure
Famous Quotation:
"When enough is not enough, a *hedonist* is born." – Sukant Ratnaker, Indian writer

Match the word with the letter of the correct definition.

_____ haggle   (a) to irritate or annoy
_____ hallucinate   (b) dangerous
_____ harass   (c) loving pleasure
_____ hazardous   (d) a false sense of reality
_____ hedonistic   (e) to bargain and reduce cost

Fill in the blank with the best word. Each word will only be used once.

haggle   hallucinate   harass   hazardous   hedonistic

(a)   Kathy knew that driving a car in the winter storm was

_____ .

(b)   However, some of her friends _____ her to make her hurry.

(c)   After driving for hours in bad weather, Kathy was so tired she began to _____ .

(d)   Instead of traveling, Kathy wanted to return home to her fun and _____ life.

(e)   When Kathy stopped at a store, she decided to _____ over the price of the food.

201. hi·er·ar·chy [noun] From Greek *hierarakhia* ("the rule of the high priest")— a group of persons having authority

Definition: People in authority

Usage:

In the Church, the ***hierarchy*** decides the doctrines that everyone must follow.

After decades of work, he finally became a member of the ***hierarchy*** of the corporation.

Famous Quotation:

"All scientists are now under the obligation … to determine the true ***hierarchy*** of values."— Friedrich Nietzsche, German philosopher and author

202. hi·lar·i·ous [adjective] From Greek *hilaros* ("cheerful")— very happy

Definition: Very cheerful and happy

Usage:

The jokes which the comedian told the audience were **hilarious**.

She enjoyed his humor which was always ***hilarious***.

Famous Quotation:

"Sometimes a clown's ***hilarious*** humor is a masquerade for his own hidden sadness." – Professor Charles

203. ho·mo·ge·ne·ous [adjective] From Latin *homo* ("same") + *genos* ("genetic origin")— having the same nature.

Definition: Having the same nature and characteristics

Usage:

The class was a ***homogeneous*** group of students.

His political supporters represented a ***homogeneous*** section of the population.

Humans are ***homogeneous*** as a species, but become different once they enter into separate societies.

Famous Quotation:

"We think of each other in a far more *homogeneous* way, because we know that there is something that is different from us. And when we say 'us,' it will mean as a species." – Dwight Schultz, American actor
Related word:
homogeneity [noun] The quality of everyone in the group having the same characteristics

204. hon·ey·moon [noun] honey ("sweet") + Greek *mene* ("moon" or "a month")— a month of happiness

Definition: A holiday or trip taken by a newly married couple; the first month of a marriage.
Usage:
The newly married couple had their *honeymoon* near the beautiful water of Niagara Falls.
After the election, the voters provided the new governor a *honeymoon* before they began to criticize him.
Famous Quotation:
"It was just that we had this phenomenal *honeymoon* relationship that just kept on going." – James Levine, American musician

205. hor·ror [noun, adjective] From Latin *horrere* ("to shudder with fear")— intense feeling of fear

Definition: A strong feeling of fear or repugnance
Usage as a noun:
When she walked through the cemetery, she felt a sense of fear and *horror*.
She tried to imagine the feeling of *horror* of the people who were on the sinking Titanic.
Famous Quotation:
"We make up *horrors* to help us cope with the real ones." – Stephen King, American writer
Usage as an adjective:
The young boys enjoyed going to *horror* movies and getting scared.
Related word:
horrible [adjective] Terrible to see or hear

Match the word with the letter of the correct definition.

_____ hierarchy   (a) the same characteristics

_____ hilarious   (b) first month of a marriage

_____ homogenou   (c) a feeling of fear

_____ honeymoon   (d) very funny

_____ horror   (e) group having authority

Fill in the blank with the best word. Each word will only be used once.

hierarchy   hilarious   homogenous   honeymoon   horror

(a)   It was a _____ group of students, since they all came from the same country.

(b)   The jokes the students told were _____ .

(c)   The class set up its own _____, based on the students with the highest test scores.

(d)   The teacher told the class the first few weeks would be a _____, compared to the work they would do later.

(e)   The way some of the students dressed with terrible clothing was like a _____ show.

206. hov·er [verb] From Middle English *hove* (" in the air")— to float in the air

Definition: To remain floating in the air

Usage:

The airplane *hovered* over the airport, waiting for an opportunity to land.

Like a mother bird, she *hovered* over her sick child.

Famous Quotation:

"The airs that *hover* in the summer sky are all asleep tonight." – William Cullen Bryant, American poet and journalist

207. hu·mil·i·ate [verb] From Latin *humiliatio* (" to make humble")— to lower someone's pride, dignity or self-respect

Definition: To deliberately lower someone's pride or self-respect

Usage:

She was *humiliated*, when people laughed at her because her dress was torn.

He tried to *humiliate* his adversary, by calling him bad names.

Famous Quotation:

"Do not *humiliate* people. Shame is a lifetime lasting effect that can be nursed, but never cured." – Fort Free, American writer

Related words:

humility [noun] Being without pride

humiliation [noun] The act of lowering someone's pride

208. hy·drate [verb] From Greek *hydor* ("water")— to provide with water

Definition: To provide with water

Usage:

The plants in the hot summer sun had to be *hydrated*.

When the people crossed the burning desert, they needed to be *hydrated*.

Famous Quotation:

"When you exercise, it is important to stay **hydrated**." – Medical advice

Related word:

dehydrated [adjective] To be <u>without</u> water. (The *opposite* of **hydrated**.)

209. hyp·o·crite [noun] From Greek *hypokrites* ("stage actor" … *Hypokrites*, of ancient Greece, was the first actor in Western history)— someone who acts or pretends

Definition: Someone who pretends, or who claims to believe something that he doesn't really believe

Usage:

The author told his audience, "Most politicians in Washington are **hypocrites**, like Hollywood actors on stage … always pretending they are someone else."

"Don't be a **hypocrite**, and pretend you are someone you are not," the father told his son.

Famous Quotation:

"The only thing worse than a liar - is a liar who is also a **hypocrite**." – Tennessee Williams, American writer

Related words:

hypocritical [adjective] The quality of pretending to be someone different than you are

hypocrisy [noun] The act of pretending about your ideas or feelings

Famous Quotation using the noun:

"**Hypocrisy**, the lie, is the true sister of evil, intolerance, and cruelty." – Raisa M. Gorbachev

210. hy·poth·e·sis [noun] From Greek *hypotithenai* ("to suppose")— a temporary explanation

Definition: A tentative and temporary explanation that can be tested against facts

Usage:

To explain the rapid spread of typhoid fever, Doctor Wright developed a **hypothesis**.

148

The famous astronomer, Carolyn Shoemaker, developed a *hypothesis* about comets.

Famous Quotation:

"The great tragedy of science is the slaying of a beautiful *hypothesis* by an ugly fact." – Thomas Huxley, English biologist and educator

Match the word with the letter of the correct definition.

_____ hover	(a) to float in the air
_____ humiliate	(b) someone who pretends
_____ hydrate	(c) a temporary explanation
_____ hypocrite	(d) provide with water
_____ hypothesis	(e) to lower someone's pride

Fill in the blank with the best word. Each word will only be used once.

hover   humiliated   hypocrite   hydrated   hypothesis

(a)   Everyone knew Robert was a _____, who would say anything to get elected.

(b)   When Julia made a big mistake, she felt _____.

(c)   The helicopter full of reporters decided to _____ over the crowd.

(d)   In the desert heat, it was necessary to stay _____ .

(e)   Galileo developed a _____ to explain the movements of the planets.

Professor Charles Explains

Why We Say: *Hot Headed*

An expression based on the idea that anger generates additional blood flow to the brain, causing heat, a reddened face, and "***hot-headed***" irrational behavior.

211. hys·ter·i·cal [adjective] From Greek *hysterikos* ("suffering in the womb")— irrational

Definition: Suffering a physical or mental pain without an organic cause; uncontrollable emotions

Usage:

When her child became deathly sick, she became ***hysterical*** and couldn't even talk.

They laughed with their entire body, because the jokes were so ***hysterical***.

Famous Quotation:

"Trying to express yourself to the press is often like arguing with an ***hysterical*** person." – Ezra Koenig, American musician

Related word:

hysteria [noun] A mental sickness without a physical or organic reason; uncontrollable emotions

212. i·de·al·is·tic [adjective]   From French *idéalism* ("to see something in a perfect form")— seeing things as being perfect

Definition: Seeing something as nice, or even perfect

Usage:

She was very ***idealistic***, and only saw the good in everything she experienced.

He was an ***idealistic*** teacher, and hoped that all of his students would love to learn.

Famous Quotation:

"Being ***idealistic*** really helps you overcome some of the obstacles put in your path." – Andy Hertzfeld, American computer scientist who helped create Apple-Macintosh

Related words:

ideal [noun] Something in a perfect form

idealism [noun] The condition of seeing things in a perfect way

idealist [noun/person] Someone who acts as though things will be perfect

213. il·lit·er·ate [adjective] From Latin *illiteratus* ("uneducated")—
cannot read letters
Definition: Not able to read or write
Usage:
Because he was **illiterate**, he could not even read the instructions to fix the machine.
The professor decided to teach all of the **illiterate** students on the ship.
Famous Quotation:
"As centuries of dictators have known, an **illiterate** crowd is the easiest to rule." – Alberto Manguel, Argentine-Canadian writer
Related word:
illiteracy [noun] The condition of not being able to read or write
[Opposite word: **literate** Being able to read and write]

214. im·pact [noun] From Latin *impactus* ("to push into")— contact by force
Definition: A violent collision of two bodies
Usage:
When the asteroid hit the earth, there was a violent **impact**.
When the two cars collided, they created an enormous **impact**.
The professor's speech had a major **impact** on the audience.
Famous Quotation:
"No one knows for certain how much **impact** they have on the lives of other people." – Jay Asher, American writer

215. im·ple·ment [noun, verb] From Latin *implere* ("to complete")— a tool; to finish something
Definition: (noun) A tool; (verb) To do what is necessary to complete a task
Usage as a noun:
To plant the seeds, the farmer used a new farming **implement** to dig holes.
Usage as a verb:
He decided to **implement** the plans, which they had agreed to perform.

It was necessary to *implement* the policies, which the president had ordered.

Famous Quotation:

"You make progress by *implementing* ideas." – Shirley Hufsteddler, American judge and educator

Related words:

implementation [noun] The act of doing something to complete a task

Match the word with the letter of the correct definition.

_____ hysterical	(a) not able to read or write
_____ idealistic	(b) a collision of two bodies
_____ illiterate	(c) having a mental problem
_____ impact	(d) to do what is necessary
_____ implement	(e) seeing things as perfect

Fill in the blank with the best word. Each word will only be used once.

hysterical   idealistic   illiterate   impact   implement

(a)   The students could not read or write, because they were all

_____ .

(b)   The teacher was _____ , and believed she could improve the lives of the students.

(c)   The friendliness of the teacher made a big _____ on the students.

(d)   To _____ the computer program, the school bought iPads for all students.

(e)   When the students received their new iPads, they became _____ with joy.

216. im·pli·cate [verb] From Latin *implicare* ("to involve, entangle")— to involve or connect

Definition: To get someone else involved, or to say that someone is involved

Usage:

He *implicated* his friends in a robbery that he committed.

Even though she was in another city at the time, witnesses said she was *implicated*.

She told the professor that her fellow students were **implicated** in the research.

Famous Quotation:

"When millions of people are starving, everyone is *implicated*." – Albert Camus, French journalist and author

Related words:

implication [noun] The condition of being involved in something

217. im·plic·it [adjective] From Latin *implicare* ("entangled")— understood indirectly

Definition: Understood, even though not directly stated or expressed

Usage:

Her anger was *implicit* in the tone of her loud voice.

The team had *implicit* confidence in the wisdom of their coach.

Famous Quotation:

"A piece of advice always contains an *implicit* threat, just as a threat always contains an *implicit* piece of advice." – Jose Bergamin, Spanish writer

imply [verb] To suggest something, without saying it

Usage:

When he told her what should be done, he **implied** that she should do it.

The way he spoke **implied** that he was involved.

Famous Quotation:

"The brotherhood of men does not **imply** their equality. Even families have fools for sons, as well as men of genius." – Aldous Huxley, English philosopher and writer

218. im·pov·er·ish [verb] From Latin *pauper, pau-paros*
("producing little")— to make poor
Definition: To reduce someone to poverty
Usage:
If you do not allow someone to work, you help to **impoverish** him.
To prevent children from learning is to **impoverish** their minds.
Famous Quotation:
"To reject art is to **impoverish** yourself." – William Rotsler, American
artist and author
Related words:
impoverishment [noun] The condition of being poor

219. im·pro·vise [verb] From Latin *in* ("not") + *providere* ("to
prepare")… [not prepared]— to invent quickly
Definition: To create or compose quickly
Usage:
They had to **improvise**, and use whatever clothes they had for the
event.
The writers were asked to **improvise**, and write a short political
speech.
Famous Quotation:
"**Improvise**, adapt, and overcome." – Clint Eastwood, American movie
producer, director and actor
Related word:
improvisation [noun] The result of someone doing something not
planned in advance

220. im·pul·sive [adjective] From Latin *impulsus* ("a quick
pressure")— to act quickly, without carefully thinking
Definition: To act without thinking
Usage:
He was very **impulsive**, always acting before thinking.
With her **impulsive** nature, she rushed into bad relationships.

Famous Quotation:

"Mature workers are less *impulsive*, less reactive, more creative and more centered." – Deepak Chopra, Indian-American author

Related word:

impulse [noun] A hidden force, or sudden wish, to do something

Match the word with the letter of the correct definition.

_____ implicate   (a) to make poor

_____ implicit   (b) to create quickly

_____ impoverished   (c) to get someone involved

_____ improvise   (d) to act without thinking

_____ impulsive   (e) understood indirectly

Fill in the blank with the best word. Each word will only be used once.

implicate   implicit   impoverished   improvise   impulsive

(a)   If people do not have any money, they are

_____ .

(b)   When the chef did not have the right tools to cook, she had to

_____ .

(c)   The young boy was _____ ,and grabbed some food before it was cooked.

(d)   When his mother saw him, he tried to _____ his sister in his bad behavior.

(e)   The mother's anger was _____ in the way she spoke.

221. in·au·gu·rate [verb] From Latin *augur* ("high priest in ancient Rome")— to induct into a high office by a religious ceremony

Definition: To place into a high office by a formal ceremony; also, to begin a new program

Usage:

People elected to an official office are often ***inaugurated*** on their first day of work.

The time came to ***inaugurate*** the new president, the man who won the national election.

The principal of the school ***inaugurated*** the new sports facility.

Related word:

inauguration [noun] The act of elevating someone new to a high office, or a new building

Usage as a noun:

"On the day of his ***inauguration***, the president of the United States takes an oath to faithfully execute the laws." – Jim Sensenbrenner, American Congressman

222. in·cen·tive [noun] Late Latin *incendere* ("to kindle" – a fire)— ignite a passion

Definition: A reward, or threat, to promote some action

Usage:

The manager promised his employees an ***incentive***, if they finished the project on time.

As an ***incentive*** to the students who received good grades, they received a field trip to a museum.

In the military, one ***incentive*** is to shoot anyone who deserts his post in time of battle.

Famous Quotation:

"Call it what you want. ***Incentives*** are what get people to work harder." – Nikita Khrushchev, First Secretary of the Communist Party of the Soviet Union

Related word:

incentivize [verb] To give someone a reason to do something

223. in·ci·dent [noun] From Latin *in* ("on") + *cadere* ("to fall")— an event

Definition: An event, that often happens without any plan

Usage:

The automobile accident was a tragic *incident*.

There was a shouting *incident* at the nightclub.

Famous Quotation:

"I think the difference between me and other people is that when I hear of an historical *incident*, I immediately write it down and Google it." – Emma Donoghue, Irish-Canadian playwright and author

Related word:

incidental [adjective] Accidental; not important

224. in·co·her·ent [adjective] From Latin *in* ("not") + *cohere* ("to stick together")— cannot stay together

Definition: Unable to think or express a thought in a clear manner

Usage:

The stories they told the police were *incoherent*, and no one could understand them.

The man in the mental institution was completely *incoherent*.

Famous Quotation:

"Dreams are nothing but *incoherent* ideas." – Benjamin Rush, one of the Founding Fathers of the United States, and an educator

Related word:

incoherence [noun] Something which is not intelligible or not understandable

225. in·com·pe·tent [adjective] From Latin *in ("not")* + *competent* (sufficient")— unable to do something right

Definition: Not qualified

Usage:

They were *incompetent* for the job we needed them to do.

Because he was *incompetent*, he did not know what to do.

Related word:

incompetence [noun] The quality of not being able to do something right

Famous Quotation:

"Never ascribe to malice that which is adequately explained by ***incompetence***." – Napoleon Bonaparte, French emperor

Match the word with the letter of the correct definition.

_____ inaugurate   (a) something which happens

_____ incentive   (b) to place into a high office

_____ incident   (c) unclear, and without logic

_____ incoherent   (d) unable to do something right

_____ incompetent   (e) a reward or threat

Fill in the blank with the best word. Each word will only be used once.

inaugurate   incentive   incident   incoherent   incompetent

(a)   Some people wanted to _____ the new president at their next meeting.

(b)   The old president gave a speech that was so _____ nobody understood it.

(c)   It was obvious that the old president was _____, and did not know what to do.

(d)   The old president's lack of ability was an _____ to vote against him.

(e)   Some voters were upset, and so they caused a loud and noisy _____ .

226. in·dis·pen·sa·ble [adjective] From Latin *in* ("not")
dispensabilis ("to disburse, distribute")— should not be distributed
Definition: Absolutely necessary to keep
Usage:
Living in the forest, he regarded his knife as an *indispensable* tool.
For learning the meaning of words, the dictionary is an *indispensable*
book.
Famous Quotation:
"Leadership and learning are *indispensable* to each other." – John F.
Kennedy, American president
Related word:
indispensability [noun] The condition of being necessary

227. in·dis·put·a·ble [adjective] From Latin *in* ("not") + *disputare*
("to weigh")— beyond dispute; beyond any argument
Definition: Without any doubt
Usage:
The facts of the matter were *indisputable*, and no one could really
question them.
It was *indisputable*, that he was the fastest man in the race.
Famous Quotation:
"One reason why mathematics enjoys special esteem, above all other
sciences, is that its laws are certain and *indisputable*." – Albert
Einstein, American scientist
Related word:
dispute [noun, verb] A disagreement, or to disagree (opposite of
indisputable)

228. in·dus·tri·ous [adjective] From Latin *industria* ("diligence,
activity")—being active Definition: Working hard to accomplish
something
Usage:
She is very *industrious,* and she always does the work she is required
to do.

He performed his tasks in an *industrious* way, constantly trying to improve his work.

Famous Quotation:

"I was obliged to be *industrious*. Whoever is equally *industrious* will succeed equally well." – Johann Sebastian Bach, German composer and musician

Related words:

industry [noun] A large business that produces items for customers

industrial [adjective] Pertaining to a large business activity

229. in·fer·ence [noun] From Latin *inferre* ("bring into")— drawing a logical conclusion from what is known

Definition: Reaching a logical conclusion from facts that are already known

Usage:

Because she was wearing the school clothing, the logical *inference* was that she was supporting that college's team.

Since he was holding her hand, the immediate *inference* was that they were together as a couple.

Famous Quotation:

"People who have given us their confidence believe they have a right to ours. The *inference* is false, since a gift confers no rights." – Friedrich Nietzsche, German philosopher and author

Related word:

infer [verb] To draw a logical conclusion from some set of facts.

230. in·fin·i·tes·i·mal [adjective] From Latin *in* ("not") + ("infinity")+ *finitus* ("a limit")— immeasurably minute (small)

Definition: Too small to be measured

Usage:

The spot on her dress was almost *infinitesimal*, it was so small.

The possibility of finding out what happened before the Big Bang is *infinitesimal*.

Famous Quotation:

"The present theory of physics ... allows space to go down into *infinitesimal* distances." – Richard P. Feynman, American theoretical physicist

Related words:

infinity [noun] Having no boundaries

Match the word with the letter of the correct definition.

_____ indispensible   (a) working hard
_____ indisputable   (b) absolutely necessary
_____ industrious   (c) deriving a conclusion from the
facts
_____ inference   (d) too small to be measured
_____ infinitesimal   (e) without any doubt

Fill in the blank with the best word. Each word will only be used once.

indispensible   indisputable   industrious   inference   infinitesimal

(a)   Daniel is always working, and is the most _____ employee in the company.

(b)   The fact that Daniel works so hard is _____, and everyone agrees.

(c)   Daniel even sees details that are so small they are _____ .

(d)   Daniel can draw an _____ from whatever he hears, and then do what is best.

(e)   Everyone agrees that Daniel is _____, and every effort should be made to keep him.

Professor Charles Explains

Why We Say: *On the Hot Seat*

In Medieval times, a suspect was placed on a metal seat of heated spikes until he confessed.

163

231. in·flu·ence [noun] From Latin *in* ("into") + *fluere* ("to flow"... like water)— a silent power not seen

Definition: Helping to direct someone, often silently

Usage:

The president's advisors have a lot of ***influence*** on his decisions.

His wife has a great amount of ***influence*** on what he does.

Famous quotation:

"A teacher affects eternity. He can never tell where his ***influence*** stops." – Henry Adams, American historian

Related word:

influential [adjective] The quality of being able to direct someone

232. in·fla·tion [noun] From Latin *inflare* ("to blow up")— the act of expanding

Definition: Expanding

Usage:

For the main event, he was responsible for the ***inflation*** of the balloons.

Inflation is when the government expands the money supply by printing more and more money, and thereby reduces its value.

Famous quotation:

"By a continuing process of ***Inflation***, the government can confiscate, secretly and unobserved, an important part of the wealth of its citizens." – John Maynard Keynes, English economist

Related word:

inflate [verb] To expand or increase the size of something

233. in·gen·i·ous [adjective] From Latin *in* ("in") + *gignere* ("to give birth")—born with talent and imagination.

Definition: Having natural intelligence and imagination

Usage:

He had a natural intelligence, and his approach to solving the problem was ***ingenious***.

The human body is an *ingenious* combination of organs, plumbing, and brains which work together.

Famous quotation:

"Literature is an avenue to glory, ever open for those *ingenious* men who are deprived of honors or of wealth." – Isaac D'Israeli, British scholar and author

Related word:

ingenuity [noun] The quality of having natural talent and creativity

234. in·her·ent [adjective] From Latin *in* ("in") + *haerere* ("to stick")— an essential part of something

Definition: Something deep inside, and intrinsic

Usage:

The *inherent* purpose of the American Constitution is to allow people to live their lives freely.

In any profession we choose, there are *inherent* challenges and opportunities.

Famous Quotation:

"The *inherent* vice of capitalism is the unequal sharing of blessings. The *inherent* vice of socialism is the equal sharing of misery." – Winston Churchill, British Prime Minister and author

235. in·her·it [verb] From Latin *in* ("in") + *heres* ("heir")— to receive something because you are an heir.

Definition: To receive property from an ancestor by legal means

Usage:

The children *inherited* a large farm from their grandparents.

The boy *inherited* a lot of money from his father.

Famous Quotation:

"Blessed are the meek, for they shall *inherit* the earth." – Matthew 5:5

Related word:

inheritance [noun] The property received from an ancestor

Match the word with the letter of the correct definition.

_____ influence   (a) to expand

_____ inflation   (b) an essential part

_____ ingenious   (c) to receive from an ancestor

_____ inherent   (d) having natural talent

_____ inherit   (e) a silent power

<u>Fill in the blank with the best word. Each word will only be used once.</u>

influence   inflation   ingenious   inherent   inherit

(a)   Congress has the problem of developing a plan to reduce
_____ which is hurting the economy.

(b)   These internal economic problems are _____ in any
economy.

(c)   It was important not to let the next generation
_____ these problems.

(d)   Everyone thought the president's plan was an
_____ way to address the problem.

(e)   The president has much _____ with the people in
the Congress; so he gave them a plan.

236. in·hib·it [verb] From Latin *inhibere* ("to hold back")— to hold back

Definition: To restrain, or hold back, or prevent an act

Usage:

She tried to *inhibit* the government from imposing new taxes on the people.

Most people feel *inhibited* about doing something bad in public.

If you don't have a plan, it *inhibits* your ability to become successful.

Famous Quotation:

"Continuing to cling to the patterns you know *inhibits* your ability to discover what you don't know." – Eric Allenbaugh, American author and lecturer

Related word:

inhibition [noun] Something which tries to prevent an action

Usage as a noun:

To perform certain movie roles, many actors have to get rid of some of their *inhibitions*.

237. in·i·tia·tive [noun] From Latin *initiare* ("to begin")— beginning something

Definition: To begin something without being asked

Usage:

She took the *initiative* to set up a new clothing company.

When the house needed repairs, he took the *initiative* to do it himself.

Famous Quotation:

"*Initiative* is doing the right thing without being told." – Victor Hugo, French writer

Related word:

initiate [verb] To begin something

238. in·ject [verb] From Latin *iniectus* ("to throw in")— to throw something forcefully

Definition: To insert something forcefully

Usage:

The doctor had to *inject* the medicine into the boy with a needle.

The lawyer constantly tried to *inject* his opinions into the conversation.

Famous Quotation:

"If you ever *inject* truth into politics, you no longer have politics." –
Will Rogers, American humorist

Related word:

injection [noun] The process of inserting something

239. in·no·vate [verb] From Latin *innovare* ("to renew")— to begin
something new

Definition: To begin something new

Usage:

Leaders *innovate*, and followers imitate.

The company must *innovate*, and create some new products.

Related word:

innovation [noun] Something new which was created

Famous Quotation:

"Creativity is thinking up new things. **Innovation** is doing new things."
– Anonymous

240. in·quire [verb] From Latin *in* ("in") + *quaerere* ("ask")— to ask
a question

Definition: To seek information by asking a question

Usage:

He *inquired* from the travel bureau how long it would take to fly to
London.

Once they were lost, they had to *inquire* to find the directions.

Related word:

inquiry [noun] The act of asking for information

Famous Quotation:

"It is error only, and not truth, which shrinks from **inquiry**." – Thomas
Paine, American revolutionary and writer

Match the word with the letter of the correct definition.

_____ inhibit   (a) to create something new

_____ initiative   (b) to hold back

_____ inject   (c) the willingness to begin

_____ innovate   (d) to ask a question

_____ inquire   (e) to insert something forcefully

Fill in the blank with the best word. Each word will only be used once.

inhibit   initiative   inject   innovate   inquire

(a)   David wanted to _____ about the new product the company was creating.

(b)   It was a chance for David to _____ , and create something special.

(c)   David decided to take the _____ and make some suggestions.

(d)   David knew there were many experienced people at the company, but that did not _____ him.

(e)   David wanted to _____ her ideas into the discussion.

241. in·no·cent [adjective] From Latin *innocentem* ("harmless")— free from any blame

Definition: Free from any blame or guilt

Usage:

The judge decided that the man was ***innocent***, and had done nothing wrong.

"You are not as ***innocent*** as you say," the mother said with a smile to her children who were covered with mud.

Famous Quotation:

"It's better to risk freeing a guilty man, then to condemn an ***innocent*** one." – Voltaire, French philosopher and author

Related word:

innocence [noun] Freedom from blame

242. in·scrip·tion [noun] From Latin *in* ("on") + *scribere* ("to write")— something written

Definition: Something written, or engraved in stone

Usage:

There was an ***inscription*** on the hospital window, asking people to be silent.

The ancient Egyptian tomb has an ***inscription*** on it, warning people they may die if they open it.

Famous Quotation:

"Let there be no ***inscription*** upon my tomb. No man can write my epitaph." – Robert Emmet, Irish nationalist and orator

Related words:

inscribe [verb] To write something

script [noun] Something in writing

scripture [noun] Sacred writings

Usage:

"The Holy Scriptures are letters from heaven." – Augustine of Hippo

243. in·sight [noun] From Middle Dutch *insicht* ("to see into")—
mental vision
Definition: Able to see the hidden nature of things
Usage:
He had an *insight* into issues which no one thought about.
With her *insight*, she could see many different sides of a problem.
Famous Quotation:
"A moment of *insight* is worth a life of experience." – Oliver Wendell
Holmes, Sr., American author and professor
Related word:
insightful [adjective] Able to see the nature of things

244. in·stall [verb] From Medieval Latin *installare* ("to put in
place")— to put into position
Definition: To put something (or someone) into position.
Usage as a verb:
The carpenter decided to *install* a new door in the house.
The Vatican had to *install* a new bishop to replace the one who died.
Famous Quotation:
"Everyone must *install* his own personal set of values by which to live."
– Professor Charles
Related word:
installation [noun] Something or someone put into a position
Usage as a noun:
They built a major electrical power **installation** for the city.

245. in·te·grate [verb] From Latin *integrare* ("make whole")— to
make into one unit. Definition: To combine various people (or things)
into one complete society (or unit)
Usage:
Part of the purpose of the civil rights movement was to *integrate*
various ethnic groups into one society.
The boss wanted to *integrate* his new ideas into the company.

An *integrated* circuit in a computer is a group of electronic circuits, combined onto a small plate called a 'chip' of material, usually silicon.

Related word:

integration [noun] The condition of a group being combined

Usage as noun:

"The natural evolution of a well-educated population is *integration*." – Stacey Dash, American actress

Match the word with the letter of the correct definition.

_____ innocent	(a) something written
_____ inscription	(b) to set in position
_____ insight	(c) mental understanding
_____ install	(d) to combine
_____ integrate	(e) free from blame

Fill in the blank with the best word. Each word will only be used once.

innocent   inscription   insight   install   integrate

(a)   William wrote the _____ on a banner at the school.

(b)   It was an _____ slogan, which did not offend anyone.

(c)   It gave the principal an _____ into what the students wanted.

(d)   The principal decided to _____ new computers immediately.

(e)   It was also important to _____ new teachers into the faculty.

246. in·teg·ri·ty [noun] From Old French *integrité* ("wholeness")— honesty

Definition: Having high ethical standards of honesty and truthfulness

Usage:

She had the ***integrity*** to tell the truth, even though some people would be upset.

When people become powerful, they often lose their ***integrity***.

Famous Quotation:

"The greatness of a man is not in how much wealth he acquires, but in his ***integrity***." – Bob Marley, Jamaican musician

247. in·ten·si·fy [verb] From Middle English *in* ("in" or "toward") + *tensus* ("strain")— to increase tension

Definition: To apply power to do something

Usage:

The police had to ***intensify*** their search for the missing boy.

The press decided to ***intensify*** its coverage of the political campaign.

Famous Quotation:

"If we ***intensify*** our positive feelings, the negative ones will silently slip away." – Professor Charles

Related words:

intense [noun] Extreme pressure, physical or emotional

248. in·ten·tion·al [adjective] From Old French *entencion* ("on purpose")— on purpose

Definition: Done deliberately, not by accident

Usage:

It was not an accident, since it was ***intentional***.

Everything he does is ***intentional***, because he thinks about his actions in advance.

Famous Quotation:

"You never climb a mountain by accident. It has to be ***intentional***," – Mark Udall, American Senator

Related words:

intent, intention [nouns] The act of deliberately doing something
<u>Usage as a noun</u>:
It was her **intention** to make the trip to Paris.

249. in·ter·ac·tive [adjective] From Latin *inter* ("between") + *actus* ("doing")— acting with each other

<u>Definition</u>: Acting together with something or someone
<u>Usage</u>:
It was an ***interactive*** group of students, who did many things together.
The video games are ***interactive***, and allow the players to communicate with the television.
<u>Famous Quotation</u>:
"The best teacher is very ***interactive***." – Bill Gates, Founder of Microsoft
<u>Related word</u>:
interaction [noun] The process when doing things together

250. in·ter·cept [verb] From Latin *intercipere* ("to take or seize")— to interrupt

<u>Definition</u>: To stop, or interrupt, or take control of something
<u>Usage</u>:
The football player ***intercepted*** the pass from the opposing team.
The fighter plane ***intercepted*** the enemy aircraft.
<u>Famous Quotation</u>:
"I have nothing to ask but that you move to the other side, that you may not, by ***intercepting*** the sunshine, take from me something which you cannot give." – Diogenes, ancient Greek philosopher
<u>Related words</u>:
interception [noun] The act of interrupting and taking control

Match the word with the letter of the correct definition.

_____ integrity   (a) doing something deliberately

_____ intensify   (b) to interrupt and take control

_____ intentional   (c) honesty

_____ interactive   (d) doing something with someone

_____ intercept   (e) to add power to do something

Fill in the blank with the best word. Each word will only be used once.

integrity   intensify   intentional   interactive   intercept

(a)   Heath did not do it by accident, since what he did was

_____ .

(b)   No one objected, since everyone knows Heath is a man of
_____ and honesty.

(c)   Heath's enthusiasm for the team inspires everyone to
_____ their efforts.

(d)   Heath wants to _____ the school bus before it
reaches the park.

(e)   This is going to be an _____ effort, by all of the
people involved.

Professor Charles Explains

Why We Say: *June Bride*

In medieval England the first spring bath was in May. Clean for the first time in months, it was a good time for a girl to marry and be a "**June Bride**."

251. in·ter·dict [verb, noun] From Latin *inter* ("between") + *dicere* ("to speak")— to prohibit speaking, or to place under a legal or ecclesiastical (church) sanction

Definition: To stop or forbid

Usage as a verb:

The FBI *interdicted* the spies, before they could pass the nation's secrets to the enemy.

The Customs and Border Control tries to *interdict* things that are smuggled into the country.

interdict [noun] An order to stop people from doing something

Usage as a noun:

In Catholic canon law an *interdict* has stopped certain people from being involved in Church functions.

Famous Quotation:

"In 1208, Pope Innocent III put England under an **interdict**, which meant that all churches were locked and no services held." – *Rise of Nation State England*

252. in·ter·face [verb, noun] Latin *inter* ("between") + Modern English *face* ("face")— to have two faces touching each other

Definition: Two things or two people facing, or directly touching, each other

Usage as a verb:

The two computers had to *interface*, in order to exchange the information.

He tried to *interface* with the other people, in order to develop an understanding.

Usage as a noun:

Those who designed the *interface* for Apple systems were very intelligent people.

Famous Quotation:

"Once the product's task is known, design the *interface* first. Then implement to the *interface* design." – Jef Raskin, American computer scientist, original founder of Macintosh

253. in·ter·me·di·ate [adjective, verb] From Latin *inter* ("between") + *medius* ("in the middle")— a middle step between two extremes

Definition: To be in the middle

Used as an adjective:

There are many **intermediate** positions, between being a beginner and becoming an expert.

Students have to learn the **intermediate** steps, before they can learn the final steps.

Usage as a verb:

The coaches had to **intermediate** in the argument between the players.

When the tension between the two countries grew, the United Nations tried to **intermediate**.

Famous Quotation:

"It is easy to ignore responsibility, when one is only an **intermediate** link in a chain of action." – Stanley Milgram, American social psychologist and author

Related words:

intermediary [noun/person] Someone who helps resolve a problem by getting in between the people in conflict

254. in·ter·vene [verb] From Latin *inter* ("between") + *venire* ("to come")— to come in between

Definition: To step in between two or more people or groups, to help solve a problem

Usage:

The argument between the young girls was becoming loud, so the teacher decided to **intervene**.

He would have obtained his college degree, but military service **intervened**.

Related word:

intervention [noun] The act of coming in between to solve a problem

Famous Quotation as a noun:

"I am certain that we need a solution completely separate from military **intervention**." – Silvio Berlusconi, Prime Minister of Italy

255. in·tri·cate [adjective] From Latin *intricatus* ("entangled")— having many complicated parts
Definition: Something extremely complicated
Usage:
The inner mechanism of a watch is very *intricate*.
A government bureaucracy is an *intricate* set of laws.
Famous Quotation:
"Drawings help people to work out *intricate* relationships between parts." – Christopher Alexander, Austrian-American architect

Match the word with the letter of the correct definition.

_____ interdict	(a) to be in the middle
_____ interface	(b) to be in direct contact
_____ intermediate	(c) something very complicated
_____ intervene	(d) to prohibit from speaking
_____ intricate	(e) to go between to solve a problem

Fill in the blank with the best word. Each word will only be used once.

interdict   interface   intermediate   intervene   intricate

(a)   The United Nations had to find _____ steps to solving the problem.

(b)   The diplomatic issues were very _____ , and required careful thought.

(c)   Because the issues were so complicated, some diplomats did not want to _____ .

(d)   Some people thought it would be best to _____ the diplomats before they went to the meeting.

(e)   However, eventually the diplomats would have to _____ to resolve the matter.

256. in·trin·sic [adjective] From Latin *intrinsecus* ("internal")— concerning the inner nature of something

Definition: Pertaining to the essential (inner) nature of something

Usage:

He recognized the ***intrinsic*** value of family life.

The teacher loved the ***intrinsic*** goodness in her young students.

Famous Quotation:

"To have that sense of one's own ***intrinsic*** worth, which constitutes self-respect..." – Joan Didion, American author

257. in·trude [verb] From Latin *intrudere* ("coming uninvited")— to forcefully enter uninvited

Definition: To enter forcefully, without being invited

Usage:

They ***intruded*** into the conversation, without being invited.

The man decided to ***intrude*** into the meeting, even though he was not part of the organization.

Famous Quotation:

"How strange that nature does not knock, and yet does not ***intrude***." – Emily Dickenson, American poet

Related words:

intrusion [noun] The act of joining when not invited

intrusively [adverb] To act in an impolite way

258. in·tu·i·tion [noun] From Latin *intueri* ("to have an insight")— to understand without thinking

Definition: To understand something, without rationally thinking about it

Usage:

'Women's ***intuition***' is a phrase, meaning women understand things without being told.

His ***intuition*** told him that the man was lying.

Famous Quotation:

"*Intuition* will tell the thinking mind where to look next." – Jonas Salk, American medical researcher
Related word:
intuitive [adjective] The quality of having unusual insights

259. in·vade [verb] From Latin *invadere* ("to enter violently")— to enter by force to conquer
Definition: To enter someone else's territory by force; to conquer or pillage
Usage:
The dictator sent his army to *invade* the neighboring country.
The man came to her house and *invaded* her privacy.
Related word:
invasion [noun] The act of entering by force
Famous Quotation:
"An **invasion** of armies can be resisted, but not an idea whose time has come." – Victor Hugo, French author

260. in·va·lid [adjective, noun/person] From Latin *in* ("not") + *validus* ("strong")— not legal; not physically able
Definition: (adjective) Illegal; (noun) a disabled person
Usage as an adjective:
The document was legally *invalid*, because it did not have the correct signature on it.
It was an *invalid* passport, because the date had expired.
Usage as a noun/person:
The automobile accident broke his back and he would be an *invalid* for his entire life.
Famous Quotation:
"Someone who has the misfortune to become a physical *invalid* often has more time to develop his or her mental abilities." – Professor Charles
Related word:
invalidate [verb] To make illegal

Match the word with the letter of the correct definition.

_____ intrinsic   (a) to enter without being invited

_____ intrude   (b) to have insights

_____ intuition   (c) to enter by force

_____ invade   (d) the inner nature of something

_____ invalid   (e) not legal; disabled

Fill in the blank with the best word. Each word will only be used once.

intrinsic   intrude   intuition   invade   invalid

(a)   The Prime Minister's female _____ told her there would be a war, if she did not act.

(b)   If no action were taken, one of the countries would _____ the other country.

(c)   Many advised the Prime Minister to _____ into the existing negotiations.

(d)   Her _____ self-respect demanded that she should not remain silent.

(e)   The Prime Minister was concerned that her authority to act was legally _____ .

261. in·voke [verb] From Latin *invocare* ("to call upon, to ask")— to ask or pray

Definition: To call on a higher power for help or inspiration

Usage:

Many ancient people *invoked* the rain gods, to help them grow their crops.

Since he is having a problem with his studies, he decided to *invoke* the help of his friends.

Famous Quotation:

"Let both sides *invoke* the wonders of science, instead of its terrors." – John F. Kennedy, American president

Related word:

invocation [noun] The act of asking the gods for something. [Also, *invocation* is often a prayer service]

262. in·volve [verb] From Latin in ("*in*") + *volvere* ("to roll")— to roll into.

Definition: To become a part of something

Usage:

She wants to *involve* the younger children in the library activities.

He decided to get *involved* in the computer industry.

Famous Quotation:

"If you are not actively *involved* in getting what you want, then you don't really want it." – Peter McWilliams, American author

Related word:

involvement [noun] A part of something

263. ir·ra·tion·al [adjective] From Latin in ("not") + *rationalis* ("reason")— unreasonable

Definition: Unreasonable; not rational

Usage:

When people are angry, they often say things which are *irrational*.

Sometimes, what sounds reasonable to an ignorant person sounds *irrational* to someone who is educated.

"The advance of science spares us from *irrational* fears." – Martin Rees, British cosmologist and astrophysicist

Related word:

irrationality [noun] The act of being unreasonable

264. ir·ri·gate [verb] From Latin *irrigare* ("lead water to")— to bring water to dry land

Definition: To bring water to crops or farms

Usage:

Because of the drought, the farmers had to *irrigate* their crops.

Sandy soils do not retain water, and must be *irrigated* more often than dirt soil.

Related word:

irrigation [noun] The process of providing water

Famous Quotation using as a noun:

"Rice is grown almost wherever **irrigation** is possible." – Isabelle Bird, English traveler and author

265. i·tin·er·ar·y [noun] From Latin *itineris* ("journey")— a travel schedule

Definition: A schedule of travels

Usage:

She kept an *itinerary* of the countries she was going to visit.

Years later, he reviewed the *itinerary* of all of the travels he had done.

Famous Quotation:

"An *itinerary* of one's travels is also a record of one's mental development." – Professor Charles

Related word:

itinerate [adjective] To travel from place to place

Match the word with the letter of the correct definition.

_____ invoke   (a) to bring water

_____ involve   (b) to ask for something

_____ irrational   (c) to become a part of

_____ irrigate   (d) a travel schedule

_____ itinerary   (e) unreasonable

Fill in the blank with the best word. Each word will only be used once.

invoke   involved   irrational   irrigate   itinerary

(a)   Alicia needed to create an _____ for her trip to Egypt.

(b)   Many people in ancient Egypt were _____, and prayed to animal gods.

(c)   To bring rain for their crops, some Egyptians would _____ the thunder god.

(d)   To get water for their crops, other people preferred to _____ their farms.

(e)   In modern times farmers and their families are all _____ in helping.

266. Jan·u·ar·y [noun]

Usage:

On **January** 7, 1714 a patent was issued for the first typewriter, designed by British inventor Henry Mill.

On **January** 7, 1782 the first U.S. commercial bank was opened in Philadelphia, called the Bank of North America.

Derivative word:

Janus-faced [adjective] A two-faced person who cannot be trusted.

267. joint·ly [adverb] From Latin *iungere* ("to join")— doing something together

Definition: Doing something together with other people

Usage:

The married couple did everything *jointly*, including their bank accounts.

It was necessary for everyone on the team to do things *jointly*.

Famous Quotation:

"The earth, upon whom day and night *jointly*... shall kindly place us into ever pleasant abode." – Atharva Veda, Hindu Veda

Related word:

 join [verb] To be together

268. jour·nal·ism [noun] From Modern French *journal* ("what happens daily")— the profession of gathering and reporting the news every day

Definition: The profession of gathering and reporting the news to the public every day

Usage:

His entire family was in the field of *journalism* for generations.

Good *journalism* is important, so that the public can find out the facts of their society.

Famous Quotation:

"*Journalism* is the first rough draft of history." – Alan Barth, American journalist

Related words:
journalist [noun/person] Someone in the profession of reporting the news
journal [noun] A record, book, or newspaper

269. jus·ti·fy [verb] From Latin *iustus* ("just") *+facere* ("to do")— to prove something is right
Definition: To prove something is just and right
Usage:
He had to *justify* to his superiors the time he spent on the project.
The government had to *justify* how they spent the money from the taxpayers.
Famous Quotation:
"Those who lack courage will always find a philosophy to *justify* it."
Albert Camus, French journalist and author
Related word:
justification [noun] The act of proving that something is right

270. ju·ve·nile [noun, adjective] From Latin *iuvenilis* ("a young person")— not fully grown
Definition: (noun/person) A young person or animal; (adjective) a childish act
Usage as a noun:
Younger children, and some teen-agers, are called '*juveniles*.'
When a dog is a *juvenile*, it is called a 'puppy.'
Usage as an adjective:
Even though he was an adult, his actions were *juvenile*.
Famous Quotation:
"Many habits you acquire as a *juvenile* are the ones you carry with you for life." – Professor Charles

Why We Say: *January*

The 'door' (Latin word *ianua*) to the New Year is the month of the Roman god of beginnings, the two-faced *Janus*, who looks at the future and the past.

Match the word with the letter of the correct definition.

_____ January	(a) to prove something is right
_____ jointly	(b) the first month of the year
_____ journalism	(c) a young person
_____ justify	(c) giving people the news
_____ juvenile	(d) doing something together

Fill in the blank with the best word. Each word will only be used once.

January   jointly   journalism   justify   juvenile

(a)   Since Paul was a _____ , he could not go into the adult section of the arena.

(b)   Paul decided to go _____ with his other classmates to the younger section.

(c)   Paul did not understand how they could _____ having separate seats for adults.

(d)   In the month of _____ , the adult section had warmer seats.

(e)   Since it was an important game, many people from _____ were there to write about the game.

190

271. jux·ta·pose [verb] From Latin *iuxta* ("near") + *ponere* ("to put")— to put near

Definition: To place near something else, or side by side

Usage:

When joy is ***juxtaposed*** next to pain, it helps build character.

The writer had to ***juxtapose*** the words, in order to make the sentence more interesting.

Related word:

juxtaposition [noun] The result of moving things around

Famous Quotation:

"I like the construction of sentences and the **juxtaposition** of words – not just how they sound, or what they mean, but even what they look like." – Don DeLillo, American writer

272. *kar·ma* [noun] From Sanskrit *karma* ("action" or "fate")— the total effect of your actions (from Hinduism and Buddhism)

Definition: The total effect of your actions or conduct

Usage:

Because she is leading a good life, she thinks her ***karma*** will always be good.

You can look at him, and see that he has good ***karma***.

Famous Quotation:

"How people treat you is their ***karma***; how you react is yours." – Buddhist proverb

273. kin [noun] Old English *cynn* ("family")— one's family or relatives

Definition: Your family or relatives

Usage:

All of the people at the family reunion were his ***kin***.

She traveled across the ocean, to finally meet her ***kin*** whom she had never seen.

Famous Quotation:

"One would be in less danger from the wiles of a stranger if one's own **kin** were more fun to be with." – Ogden Nash, American writer of children's books

274. knowl·edge [noun] From Latin *gnoscere* ("to perceive a thing")— being directly and personally aware of something
Definition: The fact of having information and being personally aware of things
Usage:
He has a lot of **knowledge** on the subject of science, which he has studied for years.
Those who have **knowledge** have a much more enjoyable time in life.
Famous Quotation:
"**Knowledge** without thinking is useless; thinking without **knowledge** is dangerous." – Confucius, Chinese philosopher

275. la·ment [verb] From Latin *lamentari* ("to wail" or to cry")— to express sorrow
Definition: To express grief or sorrow
Usage:
She **lamented** the death of her parents.
The students **lamented** their bad behavior at the party.
Famous Quotation:
"It is more fitting for a man to laugh at life than to **lament** over it." – Lucius Annaeus Seneca , Roman philosopher and statesman
Related word:
lamentation [noun] Expressing sorrow, or crying

Match the word with the letter of the correct definition.

_____ juxtapose   (a) family or relatives

_____ karma   (b) being aware of something

_____ kin   (c) to express sorrow

_____ knowledge   (d) to place side by side

_____ lament   (e) the effect of your actions

Fill in the blank with the best word. Each word will only be used once.

juxtapose   karma   kin   knowledge   lament

(a)   The philosophical idea of _____ originated in India.

(b)   In India, family members and other _____ are in close harmony.

(c)   In ancient Greece, philosophers taught that "_____ is virtue."

(d)   The writers of Sanskrit in India often _____ the ideas in their books.

(e)   Many people in India are sad, and _____ that they never learned how to read.

276. la·tent [adjective] From Latin *latentem* ("lying hidden")— out of sight

Definition: Out of sight

Usage:

The forensic scientists at the police department found the *latent* fingerprints at the crime scene.

Teachers are aware that many students have *latent* talents.

Famous Quotation:

"Every experience develops some *latent* force within you." – John Heywood, English writer

277. lat·i·tude [noun] From Latin *latitudo* ("width, extent") The angular distance measured north and south of the Equator (different from **longitude**, which measures the distance from east to west of the prime meridian in Greenwich, England)— nautical distance; freedom from restraint

Definition: Distance measured north and south of the equator; also, a freedom from restraint

Usage:

(1)   To keep the ship traveling in the correct direction, the ship's captain calculated the *latitude*.

(2)   The teacher provided the students the *latitude* to write about any subject.

Famous Quotation:

"The rule of law does not restrain our freedom. On the contrary, it provides us with the *latitude* to do more things, without being attacked by others." – Professor Charles

278. lease [noun, verb] From Old French *laissier* ("to let go")— a contract allowing someone else to use your property

Definition: A contract to rent your property to someone; an opportunity to improve yourself

Usage as a noun:

The newly married couple signed a *lease*, to rent the house for two years.

After she graduated from college, she felt like she had a new *lease* on life.

Famous Quotation:

"We are only tenants on earth, and shortly the great Landlord will give us notice that our *lease* has expired." – Joseph Jefferson, American actor

Usage as a verb:

The owner was able to *lease* his house to the students, and to collect rent every month.

279. leg·a·cy [noun] From Latin *legatus* ("ambassador by a final will")— an inheritance

Definition: An inheritance; money or property given to you by someone from the past

Usage:

As a *legacy*, his father left him a farm with many animals on it.

The children had to divide the *legacy* which their parents left them.

Their ancestors left them a *legacy* of war.

Famous Quotation:

"No *legacy* is as rich as honesty." – William Shakespeare, English author and playwright

280. le·git·i·mate [adjective] From Latin *legitimare* ("to make lawful")— lawful and legal

Definition: Legal and lawful

Usage:

He had a *legitimate* claim to being the owner of the property.

When he failed to arrive at the meeting on time, he provided a *legitimate* reason.

The people elected to high office are the *legitimate* managers of the country.

Famous Quotation:

"The **legitimate** use of violence can only be that which is used in self defense." – Ron Paul, American Congressman

Match the word with the letter of the correct definition.

_____ latent   (a) a contract to rent
_____ latitude   (b) an inheritance
_____ lease   (c) out of sight
_____ legacy   (d) lawful
_____ legitimate   (e) measurement of distance

Fill in the blank with the best word. Each word will only be used once.

latent   latitude   lease   legacy   legitimate

(a)   Edward was given enough _____ to finish the document within a week.

(b)   It was an important document, since it was a _____ for Edward's new apartment.

(c)   There were some _____ markings on it, which Edward could not read easily.

(d)   To make sure it was _____ , Edward gave it to a lawyer to review.

(e)   Edward had acquired many old things as a _____ from his father.

281. li·a·bil·i·ty [noun] From Latin *ligare* ("to bind")— to be legally responsible

Definition: Legally bound and responsible; a handicap or hardship

Usage:

He could not escape the responsibility and *liability* for his actions.

His *liability* for causing the accident will cost him a lot of money.

His broken arm was a *liability*, which prevented him from playing ball.

Famous Quotation:

"We must be one thing or the other, an asset or a *liability*." – Countee Cullen, American author

Related word:

liable [adjective] To be legally responsible for something

282. lib·er·al [adjective] From Latin *liberalis* ("noble, gracious")— not limited to any traditional views

Definition: Not limited by tradition; not orthodox

Usage:

The study of *Liberal* Arts is to open the minds of students to new ideas.

He provided *liberal* portions of food, giving large amounts to everyone.

Famous Quotation:

"A *liberal* education is at the heart of a civil society, and at the heart of a *liberal* education is the act of teaching." – A. Bartlett Giamatti, American professor of English Literature and president of Yale University

283. loy·al [adjective] From Middle French *loyal* ("faithful")—being faithful

Definition: Faithful to a person, a country, or to an idea

Usage:

The soldier had always been *loyal* to his country.

The man was *loyal* to his friends, even when they had difficulties.

Famous Quotation:

"One *loyal* friend is worth ten thousand relatives." – Euripides, ancient Greek playwright

Related word:
loyalty [noun] The act of being faithful

284. lu·na·tic [noun/person; adjective] From Late Latin *lunaticus* ("moon sick") from Latin *luna* ("moon")— someone with mental problems

Definition: Someone who has mental problems; insane

Usage as a noun:

Many years ago, mental patients at psychiatric hospitals were known as *lunatics*.

Usage as an adjective:

Bedlam, the Bethlem Royal Hospital, was a *lunatic* asylum in England.

Famous Quotation:

"Every reform movement has a *lunatic* fringe." – Theodore Roosevelt, U.S. president

Related word:

lunacy [noun] The condition of doing something which is irrational

285. lux·u·ry [noun] From Latin *luxuria* ("excess, extravagance")— something not necessary but adding pleasure

Definition: Not necessary to live, but adding pleasure or comfort

Usage:

They wanted a life of *luxury*, but they were not sure how to pay for it. If you can afford to own a yacht, it means that you are living a life of *luxury*.

Famous Quotation:

"The saddest thing I can imagine is to get used to *luxury*." – Charlie Chaplin, American actor

Match the word with the letter of the correct definition.

_____ liability	(a) having mental problems
_____ liberal	(b) excessive pleasure
_____ loyal	(c) not limited to tradition
_____ lunatic	(d) to be legally bound
_____ luxury	(e) being faithful

Fill in the blank with the best word. Each word will only be used once.

liability   liberal   loyal   lunatic   luxury

(a)   Caroline has a very _____ attitude, and wants to hear his opinion.

(b)   As a soldier, Kevin was _____ to his country.

(c)   Although his wounded leg was a _____ , Kevin could still drive a car.

(d)   Because Kevin was shot in the head, some people thought he was a _____.

(e)   Soldiers know that they will never earn enough money to live a life of _____ .

Professor Charles Explains
Why We Say: *Keep Your Shirt On*

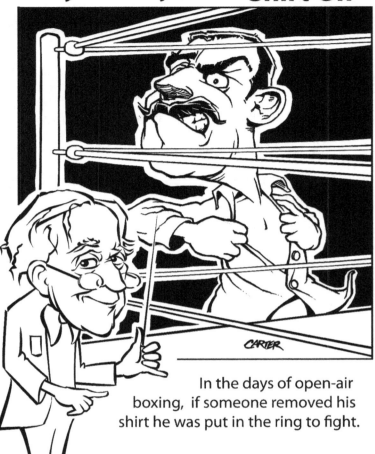

In the days of open-air boxing, if someone removed his shirt he was put in the ring to fight.

286. mag·nif·i·cent [adjective] From Latin *magnus* ("great") + *facere* ("made")—splendid in appearance.

Definition: Greatness in appearance or in conduct

Usage:

The musicians put on a ***magnificent*** performance for the audience.

There was a ***magnificent*** view from the top of the mountain.

Famous Quotation:

"Knowledge is beautiful, but wisdom is ***magnificent***." – Debasish Mridha, American physician and author

Related words:

magnificence [noun] The condition of being great in some way

287. main·tain [verb] From Old Latin *manus* ("hand")+ *tenere* ("to hold")— to hold in your hand.

Definition: To keep up, and to preserve in good condition

Usage:

The owner wanted to ***maintain*** the building in excellent condition.

In order to get into college, it is necessary for the student to ***maintain*** a high academic average.

Famous Quotation:

"If we do not ***maintain*** justice, justice will not ***maintain*** us." – Francis Bacon, English philosopher and statesman

Related word:

maintenance [noun] The act of preserving something in good condition

288. ma·lig·nant [adjective] From Latin *malignans* ("acting from malice")— something bad

Definition: Bad, malevolent, or evil

Usage:

The tumor in the man's leg was ***malignant***.

The ***malignant*** neglect of their education condemned the children to a life of ignorance.

Famous Quotation:

"How terrible it is to be a mischievous and *malignant* hypocrite." –
Voltaire, French philosopher and author
Related word:
malign [verb] To say something bad about someone
Usage as a verb:
She **maligned** him by saying bad things about him.

289. ma·nip·u·late [verb] From Latin *manus* ("hand") + *plere* ("to
fill")— to operate skillfully with your hands
Definition: To operate skillfully; to falsify information for personal gain
Usage:
The mechanic tried to *manipulate* the machinery, in order to get it to
work properly.
In order to hide his theft, the dishonest accountant *manipulated* the
numbers.
Famous Quotation:
"Some people have the power to *manipulate* the machinery of
nations, but they cannot govern their own emotions." – Professor
Charles

290. mar·gin·al [adjective] From Latin *marginalis* ("border,
margin")— at the margin.
Definition: Less important
Usage:
The company's problems were *marginal*, and did not affect the central
operations.
It was regarded as a *marginal* issue, and not related to the main
subject.
Famous Quotation:
"I think fairness means that you give equal time to every point of view
no matter how *marginal*." – Bill Keller, American writer

Match the word with the letter of the correct definition.

_____ magnificent   (a) something bad
_____ maintain   (b) not important
_____ malignant   (c) being great in some way
_____ manipulate   (d) to preserve in good condition
_____ marginal   (e) to operate skillfully

Fill in the blank with the best word. Each word will only be used once.

magnificent   maintain   malignant   manipulate   marginal

(a)   There was a _____ tumor on Tony's arm, and it required surgery.

(b)   With the pain in his arm, it was difficult for Tony to _____ the controls of the airplane.

(c)   Tony did not want to stop flying, since the scenery was _____ from the air.

(d)   The doctor told Tony to eat good food, in order to _____ his health.

(e)   Tony's health was only _____, which required that he postpone the operation.

291. mas·cu·line [adjective] From Latin *masculinus* ("from the male sex")— regarding something male

Definition: Pertaining to male, not female

Usage:

He made an effort to show how *masculine* he was, by wearing shirts which showed his muscles.

The tournament was really a *masculine* event, since there was a lot of rough activity.

Famous Quotation:

"I think of *masculine* and feminine energy as two sides of a battery." – Tracy McMillan, American author and television writer

Related word:

masculinity [noun] The condition of being male

292. max·i·mize [verb] From Latin *maximum* ("greatest")— to make as large as possible

Definition: To increase, and make as large as possible

Usage:

To *maximize* his opportunities to get a job, the student took some courses in computer science.

To *maximize* the company's profits, the president of the company introduced more technology.

Famous Quotation:

"We must expect to fail… and to *maximize* the benefit from what is learned in the process." – Ted W. Engstrom, American author

Related word:

maximum [noun] The largest possible amount

293. med·i·ta·tion [noun] From Latin *meditationem* ("thought, reflection")— to reflect

Definition: Quieting reflecting and thinking

Usage:

The Buddhists have always used *meditation* to reflect on their lives.

He spent at least 10 minutes every day in some form of *meditation*.

"Just as breathing is the life of the body, *meditation* is the life of the soul." – Bhagwan Shree Rajneesh, Indian guru and teacher

Related word:

meditate [verb] To reflect, to think carefully about life

294. mem·o·rize [verb] From Latin *memoria* ("memorize")— to commit to memory

Definition: To commit to memory

Usage:

The students had to *memorize* many poems for the examination.

Some Muslims *memorize* many passages of the Koran.

Famous Quotation:

"To know the laws is not to *memorize* their letter, but to grasp their full force and meaning." – Marcus Tullius Cicero, Roman statesman and philosopher

295. mer·chant [noun/person] From Anglo-French *marcheant* ("a merchant, shopkeeper")— someone who buys and sells goods for profit

Definition: Someone who buys and sells; a businessman

Usage:

He was a *merchant* who sold food and clothing to tourists.

Some *merchants* often work long hours.

Famous Quotation:

"The great dream *merchant*, Disney, was a success because make-believe was what everyone seemed to need in a spiritually empty land." – Arthur Erickson, Canadian architect and author

Related words:

merchandise [noun] The things which businesses sell

mercantile [adjective] Pertaining to business

Match the word with the letter of the correct definition.

_____ masculine   (a) to make as large as possible

_____ maximize   (b) to commit to memory

_____ meditation   (c) something male

_____ memorize   (d) a businessman

_____ merchant   (e) to reflect

Fill in the blank with the best word. Each word will only be used once.

masculine maximize meditation memorize merchant

(a) Stella obtained a good education in order to _____ her ability to find a good job.

(b) To prepare for her interview, Stella took the time to _____ information about the company.

(c) One of Stella's concerns is that the company has a _____ atmosphere, and she is a female.

(d) To relax before the interview, she does some _____ every day.

(e) She wants to demonstrate that she can be a good _____ , and can sell many of the company's products.

296. mer·it [noun] From Latin *meritum* ("value")— superior quality or worth

Definition: An award; value

Usage:

He deserved a ***merit*** or an award, because he did a good job.

His approach had a lot of ***merit***, since it could be applied to many situations.

Famous Quotation:

"I may succeed or fail, but I'm going to do it on the ***merit*** of my own instincts." – Ben Affleck, American actor

Related word:

meritocracy [noun] A system of government in which people succeed by their individual efforts, not by political or family relationships

297. mi·gra·tion [noun] From Latin *migrationem* ("a removal")— a movement

Definition: A large movement of animals, birds, or people from one place to another

Usage:

The geese had their annual winter ***migration*** to the warmer weather.

After many wars, a ***migration*** of refugees occurs.

Famous Quotation:

"Canadian geese are known for their seasonal ***migrations*** … and have staging and resting areas where they join up with others." – Wikipedia

Related words:

migratory [adjective] Characterized by large movements

migrate [verb] To travel to a different location

Usage as a verb:

During the winter season, millions of North American Monarch butterflies **migrate** to the warmer climate of Mexico.

298. mile·stone [noun]   From Latin *mille* ("a thousand") + (stone)
(An ancient Roman mile, about 4,860 feet, was 1,000 paces (one step with each foot), marked by a stone.)— a measurement of an advance

Definition: An important advance in someone's life
Usage:
Graduating from college was a *milestone* in her life.
He knew that getting married would be a *milestone* in his life.
Famous Quotation:
"Life isn't a matter of *milestones*, but of moments." – Rose Kennedy,
American philanthropist and socialite (mother of John F. Kennedy,
Robert Kennedy, and Ted Kennedy)

299. mi·lieu [noun] From French *milieu* ("middle place")— in the
middle of surroundings
Definition: An environment or a setting
Usage:
They created a romantic *milieu*, in order to have the right atmosphere
for the party.
It was an intellectual *milieu*, with authors and artists from all over the
world.
Famous Quotation:
"A fashionable *milieu* is one in which everybody's opinion is made up
of the opinion of all of the others." – Marcel Proust, French author

300. min·i·mum [noun] From Latin *minimum* ("smallest")— the
smallest possible
Definition: The smallest amount possible
Usage:
They did the *minimum* amount of work necessary to complete the
project.
They had a *minimum* amount of information on which to base their
decision.
Famous Quotation:
"The role of a comedian is to make the audience laugh, at a *minimum*
of once every fifteen seconds."— Lenny Bruce, American comedian
and social critic
Related word:
minimize [verb] To make smaller

208

Match the word with the letter of the correct definition.

_____ merit   (a) large movement of animals or people
_____ migration   (b) an environment
_____ milestone   (c) the least possible
_____ milieu   (d) an award
_____ minimum   (e) an important advance

Fill in the blank with the best word. Each word will only be used once.

merit   migration   milestone   milieu   minimum

(a)   The students went to Tanzania to watch the annual
_____ of the zebras and the wildebeest.

(b)   The _____ in Africa was different than any
atmosphere they had known.

(c)   Their guide told them there was a _____ of
2,000,000 zebras and wildebeest.

(d)   For many animal lovers on the trip, it was a _____ in
their professional career.

(e)   The students received a _____ for making the
journey.

301. mis·con·cep·tion [noun] From Latin *mis* ("not") +
conceptionem ("comprehend")— wrong understanding
Definition: A mistaken idea or a misunderstanding
Usage:
One *misconception* about blind people is that they have better hearing
than sighted people.
Most people have *misconceptions* about how easy the lives of kings
and queens were in history.
Famous Quotation:
"Education should prepare our minds to use its powers of reason,
rather than filling our minds with the *misconceptions* of the past." –
Bryant H. McGill, American author
Related word:
misconceive [verb] To have the wrong idea about something

302. mo·bi·lize [verb] From Latin *mobilis* ("movable") — to make
movable
Definition: To make mobile or capable of being moved
Usage:
To prepare for battle, the general had to *mobilize* the army.
The politicians had to *mobilize* the public in order to get them to vote.
Famous Quotation:
"Take the first step, and your mind will *mobilize* all of its forces to your
aid." – Robert Collier, American author
Related word:
mobile [adjective] Something which is movable

303. mod·i·fy [verb] From *modus ("measure") + faere* ("to make
")— to measure differently
Definition: To change something
Usage:
He wanted to *modify* his car, in order to add more power to the
engine.

The teacher asked the students to *modify* their essays, and make them longer.

Famous Quotation:

"In science the important thing is to *modify*, and change one's ideas as science advances." – Herbert Spencer, English biologist, anthropologist, and philosopher

Related word:

modification [noun] The result of something being changed

304. mo·tive [noun] From Latin *movere* ("to inwardly move")— a psychological need to act

Definition: A reason for doing something

Usage:

Her main *motive* to take the children to a movie is because she loves them so much.

The *motives* for the Europeans to sail to North America were to get gold, to preach the Christian gospel, and to get glory.

Famous Quotation:

"We rarely do anything with a single *motive*." – Paul David Tripp, Author and Pastor

305. mul·ti·tude [noun] From Latin *multitudo* ("a crowd")— a large number

Definition: A large number of people

Usage:

A *multitude* of people came to the annual musical event.

The Bible says that Christ fed a *multitude* of people.

Famous Quotation:

"Success covers a *multitude* of blunders." – George Bernard Shaw, Irish playwright and critic

_____ misconception   (a) to make something movable

_____ mobilize   (b) a psychological need to act

_____ modify   (c) a mistaken idea

_____ motive   (d) a large number of people or things

_____ multitude   (e) to change something

Fill in the blank with the best word. Each word will only be used once.

misconception   mobilize   modify   motive   multitude

(a)   Assad, the automobile mechanic, had to _____ the engine of the car for the race.

(b)   Winning the prize money was not the only _____ , since Assad also wanted to win the First Place trophy.

(c)   The automobile club tried to _____ as many people as possible to attend the race.

(d)   Because of the advertising, they expected a _____ of people to come.

(e)   There is a _____ that automobile mechanics are not educated, but Assad has graduated from college.

Oh, . . . Just a little trouble paying my taxes.

In 9th century Ireland the conquering Danes imposed an exorbitant nose tax (part of the census), threatening to put a knife "**through the nose**" of those who did not pay.

306. mu·ta·tion [noun] From Latin *mutare* (" to change")—
gradual change

Definition: The process of changing

Usage:

Mutation is an essential part of evolution, in plants, animals, and humans.

Many human diseases are influenced by *mutations* in the genes.

Many creatures have evolved, as a result of the *mutations* over a period of time.

Famous Quotation:

"Genetic *mutations* have always happened naturally." – James Lovelock, English scientist and author

Related word:

mutate [verb] To change gradually

307. mys·ter·y [noun] From Greek *mysterion* ("a secret rite")—
something secret

Definition: Something not easily understood

Usage:

Most religions have a *mystery* which people do not understand.

Why the house burned down is a *mystery*.

How her grandfather made his fortune is a *mystery*.

Famous Quotation:

"If I have the gift of prophecy and can fathom all *mysteries*, but do not have love, I am nothing." – St. Paul, 1 Corinthians 13:2

Related word:

mysterious [adjective] Having hidden secrets

308. na·ïve [adjective] From Latin *nativus* ("just born")— too young to know.

Definition: Having no ability to analyze

Usage:

She was *naïve* in her relationships with men.

He was *naïve* enough to think that all of the employees would follow his orders.
Famous Quotation:
"It is well for the heart to be *naïve*, but not for the mind to be." – Anatole France, French writer
Related word:
naïveté [noun]The quality of having no experience with a subject

309. neg·li·gent [adjective] From Latin *neglegere* ("to neglect")— careless

Definition: To neglect or be careless; not paying attention
Usage as an adjective:
The little boy was *negligent*, and left the refrigerator door open.
The employee is *negligent*, since he makes mistakes when he writes something.
Related words:
neglect [verb] To not pay attention to something
negligible [adjective] Not important
negligence [noun] The act of being careless
Famous Quotation used as a noun:
"**Negligence** ruins the good reputation which accuracy had raised." – Ben Jonson, English playwright and literary critic

310. night·mare [noun] In 13th century England *nigt-mare* was an evil female spirit who threatened suffocation by sitting on one's chest while sleeping; by the 16th century *nightmare* was a bad dream

Usage:
The little boy woke up in the middle of the night, because he had a *nightmare*.
Trying to survive during a tornado is a *nightmare*.
Living with a group of college boys in one house is often a *nightmare*.
Famous Quotation:
"Teamwork makes the dream work, but a vision becomes a *nightmare* when the leader has a big dream and a bad team."— John C. Maxwell, American author

Match the word with the letter of the correct definition.

_____ mutation   (a) lacking the ability to analyze

_____ mystery   (b) careless

_____ naïve   (c) something not easily understood

_____ negligent   (d) a bad dream

_____ nightmare   (e) gradual changes

Fill in the blank with the best word. Each word will only be used once.

mutation   mystery   naïve   negligent   nightmare

(a)   John has the same _____ every night.

(b)   The dream was about a wolf with a _____ which made him almost human.

(c)   Why John has this dream so often is a _____ .

(d)   A friend told John that it is _____ to think that people can explain these dreams.

(e)   John was _____ , and did not take his medicine to help him sleep.

Why We Say: *Nightmare*

In 13th century England, *nigt-mare* was an evil female spirit who threatened suffocation by sitting on one's chest while sleeping; by the16th century **nightmare** was a bad dream.

311. no·bil·i·ty [noun] From Latin *nobilitatem* ("high rank")— a class of persons of high birth or rank; having strong character
Definition: Members of an upper social class; possessing inner dignity
Usage:
Members of the royal family at the English Court are members of the **nobility**.
The knights in old England were often part of the **nobility**.
Nobility is in your character, not in the family in which you are born.
Famous Quotation:
"True **nobility** is exempt from fear." – Marcus Tullius Cicero, Roman statesman and philosopher
Related words:
noble [noun/person] A member of the **nobility**
noble [adjective] Having the quality of high standards

312. no·tion [noun] From Latin *notionem* ("an idea")— an impulse
Definition: An impulse to act, without thinking
Usage:
People usually have some **notion** of what they want to do with their lives.
She has no **notion** of what to do.
Famous Quotation:
"The law is constantly based on **notions** of morality." – Byron R. White, American, Associate Justice of the U.S. Supreme Court

313. No·vem·ber [noun]
Usage:
On **November** 19th President Abraham Lincoln delivered the Gettysburg Address.
The month of **November** is when we celebrate Thanksgiving Day.
Derivative word:
novena [noun] A period of nine days of prayer

314. nov·ice [noun/person] From Latin *novicius* ("newly arrived")— someone new Definition: Someone new to an organization or to an activity
Usage:
Since he just joined the team, he was a **novice** at the sport.

218

As a **novice**, he had to work harder to learn the techniques.

Famous Quotation:

"Man arrives as a **novice** at each stage of his life." – Nicolas Chamfort, French writer

Related word:

novitiate [noun] Time when a new nun is in training

315. nu·cle·us [noun] From Latin *nucleus* ("the kernel" of a nut)— the center

Definition: The important center around which other things are gathered

Usage:

Parents are the **nucleus** of a family.

The human cell is the **nucleus** which contains the genetic material of life.

Famous Quotation:

"The family is the **nucleus** of civilization." – Will Durant, American historian and author

Related word:

nuclear [adjective] Pertaining to the central part of something

Professor Charles Explains

Why We Say: *November*

Famous Events in November: *On November 14, 1666 Samuel Pepys in Britain recorded one of the first blood transfusions in history -- between two dogs.*

You saved my life, man.

CARTER

Having nine to start with helps.

November was the 'ninth' (*novem* in latin) month in the old Roman calendar -- then was pushed back into 11th place.

Match the word with the letter of the correct definition.

_____ nobility   (a) an impulse to act

_____ notion   (b) the central part of something

_____ November   (c) the ninth month of the year

_____ novice   (d) being of high rank

_____ nucleus   (e) someone new to an activity

Fill in the blank with the best word. Each word will only be used once.

nobility   notion   November   novice   nucleus

(a)   The Medieval _____ in the English court had contests with knights on horses.

(b)   The king and queen were the _____ of the royal family in England.

(c)   Many of the knights had the _____ of becoming famous by winning the contests.

(d)   A younger squire, who was a _____ in training, was not allowed to participate until he became a knight.

(e)   Some contests were stopped during the month of _____ , when the weather was cold.

316. nu·tri·tion [noun] From Latin *nutritionem* ("a nourishing")—
the process of nourishing
Definition: The process of nourishing
Usage:
To be strong in sports, athletes eat healthy food to get good **nutrition**.
When you have poor **nutrition**, the body can become ill very easily.
Famous Quotation:
"Just as daily food is **nutrition** for the body, daily learning is **nutrition**
for the mind." – Professor Charles
Related words:
nutritious [adjective] Providing nourishment
nutrient [noun] An ingredient in food which is a source of nourishment

317. oath [noun] From Old Irish *oeth* ("oath")— a solemn promise,
sometimes before God
Definition: A solemn pledge or promise to do something
Usage:
In the courtroom, everyone who testifies must take an **oath** that they
will tell the truth.
Doctors take an **oath** to do whatever they can to help their patients.
Famous Quotation:
 "I will abstain from all wrong-doing and harm." [Often simplified:"If
you cannot do any good, at least do no harm."] – Ancient Greek
Hippocratic **Oath** taken by medical doctors. (Hippocrates was a
physician in ancient Greece.)

318. o·bese [adjective] From Latin *obesitas* ("fatness")— fat
Definition: Extremely overweight or fat
Usage as adjective:
The children became **obese**, from eating sweet cereals and pasta since
they were very young.
If you become **obese**, it will affect your health.
Related word:
obesity [noun] To be overweight

Usage as a noun:

Obesity is a major health problem in the United States.

Famous Quotation:

"**Obesity** puts our children at risk of developing serious diseases – such as Type 2 diabetes, heart disease, and depression." – Kirsten Gillibrand, American Senator

319. ob·jec·tive·ly [adverb] From Latin *ob ("against") + iacere* ("to throw in front of")— to have the facts thrown in front of you

Definition: To see the facts – and not be influenced by your emotions

Usage:

The judge in a court must *objectively* analyze what people say.

When you know the people involved, it's hard to look at situations *objectively*.

Famous Quotation:

"No parent can look *objectively* at what their children do, because their eyes are clouded with love." – Professor Charles

Related words:

objectivity [noun] Having the ability to look at things clearly

objective [noun] Having a clear goal you want to achieve.

320. ob·nox·ious [adjective] From Latin *ob* ("toward") + *noxa* ("injury")— very unpleasant

Definition: Distasteful or unpleasant

Usage:

He was often *obnoxious*, saying things which other people found distasteful.

The little boy was *obnoxious*, because he was always shouting.

Famous Quotation:

"Learn from the rude and *obnoxious* people you meet, because they remind you how NOT to act toward others." – Professor Charles

Match the word with the letter of the correct definition.

_____ nutrition   (a) a solemn promise

_____ oath   (b) to see things clearly

_____ obese   (c) causing discomfort

_____ objectivity   (d) overweight

_____ obnoxious   (e) process of nourishing

Fill in the blank with the best word. Each word will only be used once.

nutrition   oath   obese   objectivity   obnoxious

(a)   Because Betty ate so much bad food, she became
_____ before she was a teenager.

(b)   Her weight made her angry, so Betty was often
_____ when talking to people.

(c)   The bad diet also meant that Betty had poor _____
and would become ill.

(d)   Because of their love for her, it was difficult for Betty's parents
to look at her with any _____ .

(e)   Betty's father, a doctor, took a medical _____ to
help her become healthy.

321. ob·li·ga·tion [noun] From Latin *obligationem* ("a pledge of responsibility")— a legal responsibility
Definition: A legal or moral responsibility
Usage:
The man signed a legal contract, so now he has an *obligation*.
Parents have an *obligation* to provide for the welfare of their children.
People have a moral *obligation* to tell the truth.
Famous Quotation:
"Remember that you not only have the right to be an individual, you have an *obligation* to be one." – Eleanor Roosevelt, American humanist and wife of President Franklin D. Roosevelt
Related words:
obligate, oblige [verbs] Requiring someone to have responsibility for something
obligatory [adjective] Something that is required

322. ob·tain [verb] From Latin *obtinere* ("to get and hold something")— to acquire
Definition: To acquire some property or a legal right
Usage:
The family *obtained* a new house, since the old one was too small.
He *obtained* success, by working hard and planning everything he did.
She *obtained* a college degree, through years of effort and study.
Famous Quotation:
"The important thing about science is not just to *obtain* new facts, but to discover new ways of looking at them." – William Bragg, Sr., British physicist and chemist

323. Oc·to·ber [noun]
Usage:
October is the month in which the voyage of Christopher Columbus to North America is celebrated.
Famous Quotation:

"I'm so glad I live in a world where there are **Octobers**." – L.M. Montgomery, Canadian author

Derivative words:

octopus [noun] A sea creature with eight arms

octagon [noun] An eight-sided figure

324. of·fense [noun] From Latin *offensa* (" an offence")— causing ill will or anger

Definition: Causing anger or displeasure; being aggressive

Usage:

(1)   Bad behavior is an *offence* to polite people.

She took *offense* even at the smallest criticism someone made about her.

(2)   In order to win the game, the team had to go on the *offence* against their opponent.

Famous Quotation:

"We should be too big to take *offense*, and too noble to give it." – Abraham Lincoln, American president

Related word:

offensive [adjective] Disagreeable, causing anger, or going on an attack

offend [verb] To be disagreeable or cause anger

offender [noun/person] Someone who is disagreeable or causes anger

[In the law, an **offender** is someone who commits a crime.]

325. ol·i·gar·chy [noun] From Greek *oligos* ("a few") + *arkhein* ("to rule")— **a** government which is controlled by a few people.

Definition: A small ruling class of people

Usage:

Throughout history, an *oligarchy* is usually when a group of rich people obtain power.

When career politicians in a democracy obtain power, they turn it into an *oligarchy*.

Most of the members of the *oligarchy* had contempt for the nation's ordinary citizens.

Famous Quotation:

"The tyranny of a prince in an *oligarchy* is not as dangerous to the public welfare as the apathy of a citizen in a democracy."— Charles Montesquieu, French political philosopher and author

Related words:

oligarch [noun/person] A member of a small ruling class

monarch [noun/person] Latin *monus* (one) + Greek *arkhos* (ruler)— A person who rules alone, i.e. king or queen

monarchy [noun] Latin *monus* (one) + Greek *arkein* (rule)— A government ruled by one person

anarchy [noun] From Greek *ana* (without) + *arkhos* (a ruler)— A society without a leader

Famous Events in October: *Oct. 1, 1908: the first "affordable car for people" was sold: Henry Ford's Model T*

Just about $800 dollars each! And I've sold eight cars already!

CARTER

October was the 'eighth' (*Octo* in Latin) month in the old Roman calendar - until January and February were both put in front of March.

Match the word with the letter of the correct definition.

_____ obligation   (a) to acquire something

_____ obtain   (b) causing ill will

_____ October   (c) government by a few

_____ offense   (d) the tenth month of the year

_____ oligarchy   (e) a legal or moral responsibility

Fill in the blank with the best word. Each word will only be used once.

obligation   obtain   October   offense   oligarchy

(a)   Always wanting total control, Tim tried to _____
political power.

(b)   Tim tried to cover up _____ he had committed
against relatives.

(c)   If they find out, the election officials have an
_____ to inform the public.

(d)   Some people were worried, because Tim wanted to form an
_____ .

(e)   Since it was the month of _____ , people were
preparing for the election next month.

326. op·pose [verb] From Latin *opponere* ("to put against") — to be against

Definition: To be against someone or something

Usage:

The two best footballs teams will *oppose* each other in the final match. She was *opposed* to his ideas.

Famous Quotation:

"Men often *oppose* something merely because they were not involved in planning it, or because it may have been planned by those whom they dislike." – Alexander Hamilton, American Founding Father

Related words:

opposite [adjective] On the other side of something

opposition [noun] Those who are against you

opponent [noun/person] Someone who is against you

327. op·press [verb] From Medieval Latin *ob* ("against") + *premere* ("to press hard")— to hold down by force

Definition: To hold people down by force or fear

Usage:

Throughout history kings would often *oppress* the ordinary people. Some governments *oppress* their own people.

Famous Quotation:

"Among those who dislike **oppression** are many who like to *oppress* when they have the power." – Napoleon Bonaparte, French emperor

Related words:

The oppressed [noun/people] People who are held down by those in power

oppression [noun] The act of holding people down

328. o·ver·whelm [verb] From Old English *over* ("over") + *whelmen* ("to cover ")— to cover over completely

Definition: To cover over completely

Usage:

The army has many more soldiers, and so it is easy to **overwhelm** the enemy.

She will **overwhelm** the others in the contest with many more facts than they have.

After the tragedy, the sadness **overwhelmed** her.

<u>Famous Quotation</u>:

"Enlightenment must come little by little, otherwise it will **overwhelm**." – Idries Shah, Indian-English writer

<u>Related word</u>:

overwhelming [adjective] A flood of something, for example of water, of soldiers, of emotions

329. ox·y·gen [noun] From the ancient Greek words *oxys,* ('sharp') and *genes* ('creation'), (named by French chemist Lavoisier because it is sharp and rusts metal.)— A gas that constitutes 21% of the atmosphere.

<u>Definition</u>: The gas *oxygen* is necessary for breathing

<u>Usage</u>:

Because of the fire, the lack of **oxygen** made it difficult for him to breathe.

His personality was so strong, that people said he sucked all of the **oxygen** out of the room.

<u>Famous Quotation</u>:

"What **oxygen** is to the lungs, such is hope to the meaning of life."— Emil Brunner, Swiss Protestant theologian

"Honest communication is the **oxygen** of understanding." – Professor Charles

<u>Related words</u>:

hydrogen [noun] From Greek *hydro* ("water") + *genes* ("creation"), because this gas forms water when in contact with **oxygen**

330. pac·i·fy [verb] From Latin *pacificare* ("to make peace")— to make peace

<u>Definition</u>: To ease someone's anger, or to stop someone from fighting

The armies of ancient Rome tried to *pacify* the tribes of Europe who wanted to make war.

The mother had to *pacify* her children, when they were upset.

Famous Quotation:

"A few minutes of calm meditation can *pacify* many hours of excited emotions." – Professor Charles

Related word:

pacification [noun] The process of making peace

pacifism [noun] The belief that all international disputes can be settled without war.

pacifist [noun/person] Someone who is against all war

Match the word with the letter of the correct definition.

_____ oppose   (a) a gas for breathing

_____ oppress   (b) to settle something peacefully

_____ overwhelm   (c) to hold down by force

_____ oxygen   (d) to be against

_____ pacify   (e) to cover up completely

Fill in the blank with the best word. Each word will only be used once.

oppose   oppress   overwhelm   oxygen   pacify

(a)   King Harold continued to _____ his people.

(b)   Many people were getting ready to _____ him and take power.

(c)   To stop the people, King Harold had to _____ them with an army of soldiers.

(d)   Once the king succeeded, he could _____ the population and bring peace.

(e)   In ancient days of history people did not understand gas, and so they did not know how to use _____ for underwater experiments.

331. pan·a·ce·a [noun] From Greek *pan* ("all") + *akos* ("cure")— a cure for all diseases

Definition: A cure for everything

Usage:

Many years ago people regarded aspirin as a ***panacea*** for most physical ailments.

There is no ***panacea*** for cancer.

Wealth is a ***panacea*** for poverty.

There is no ***panacea*** for unhappiness.

Famous Quotation:

"Learning is a ***panacea*** for open minds with doubts, but not for closed minds with dogmas." – Professor Charles

332. par·a·digm [noun] From Greek *para* ("beside") + *deiknynai* ("to show")— a model

Definition: A model, a prototype, or a good example

Usage:

She was a ***paradigm*** of virtue because she was honest about everything she did or said.

To help the students solve the problem, the teacher provided the class with a new ***paradigm***.

Famous Quotation:

"The first movement of a ballerina should be a ***paradigm*** of strength and authority." – Robert Gottlieb, American writer and editor

333. par·a·dox [noun] A statement that seems untrue, but is true

Usage:

It's a ***paradox*** that many people look back with nostalgia on their earlier lives which they couldn't wait to leave.

It's a ***paradox*** that if the statement "This sentence is false" is actually true, then it is actually false after all, or is it true?

Famous Quotation:

"It's a *paradox* that fools and fanatics are always so certain of themselves, and wiser people so full of doubts."— Bertrand Russell, British philosopher and Nobel Laureate
Related word:
parachute [noun] From Latin *para* (against) + French *chute* (fall)— literally, 'against a fall.'

334. par·al·lel [adjective] From Greek *para* ("beside") + *allelois* ("each other")— at an equal distance at every point
Definition: Equally distant at every point; something similar
Usage:
The driver had difficulty in *parallel* parking on the street.
The country's actions were *parallel* to what had been done so many times in history.
Famous Quotation:
"Every person has *parallel* tracks. You have your personal life and your life as an artist... or whatever else you do." – Gina Bellman, New Zealand-American actress
Related word:
parallelogram [noun] In Euclidian geometry, a figure with two pairs of parallel sides.

335. pa·ri·ah [noun/person] From Portuguese *paria* ("drummer" – at festivals of the lower castes in India)— a social outcast.
Definition: A person nobody wants around.
Usage:
Since he had a contagious disease, the city treated him like a *pariah* and kept away from his house.
He was treated like a *pariah* by many people, because of his views on politics.
Famous Quotation:
"Shortly Tom came upon the juvenile *pariah* of the village, Huckleberry Finn, son of the town drunkard." – Mark Twain, American author

Professor Charles Explains
Why We Say: *Paradox*

Everything I say is a **LIE**.

Then that would mean he's lying **RIGHT NOW**. So, he must actually be telling the truth. But if he's telling the truth, then he **IS** lying . . . .

Something which seems to be an incongruity or apparent inconsistency, or seems contrary to common opinion, but may be true. From Latin *Para* ("opposite") + *doxa* ("opinion")

236

_____ panacea   (a) a model

_____ paradigm   (b) being at an equal distance

_____ paradox   (c) a cure for everything

_____ parallel   (d) a social outcast

_____ pariah   (e) a confusing statement

Fill in the blank with the best word. Each word will only be used once.

panacea   paradigm   paradox   parallel   pariah

(a)   The Greek philosopher Socrates was a _____ of a good teacher.

(b)   It's a _____ of life, that if you go looking for happiness you may not find it, but if you do something with a purpose happiness will find you.

(c)   There is no medical _____ for unhappiness, since it comes in too many forms.

(d)   We can often find a _____ between what we do in our life and what other people have done in the past.

(e)   The bad student became a _____ in the school.

336. pa·ro·chi·al [adjective] From Latin *parochialis* ("parish")—
located in a small area called a 'parish.'
Definition: Having a limited view of things, or a narrow outlook
Usage:
People from small towns often have ***parochial*** minds.
His ***parochial*** views prevented him from having a broader vision of the world.
Famous Quotation:
"Art must be ***parochial*** in the beginning in order to be cosmopolitan in the end." – George A. Moore, Irish novelist

337. pas·sion·ate [adjective] From Greek *pathos* ("to suffer")—
having deep feelings
Definition: Having powerful emotions, good or bad
Usage:
He was ***passionate*** about the idea of marrying the woman he loved.
The entire crowd was ***passionate*** about their team winning the Olympics.
Related word:
passion [noun] The quality of having strong feelings
Famous Quotation:
"A man employs his ***passion*** when he can make no use of his reason."
– Marcus Tullius Cicero, Roman statesman and philosopher

338. pa·ter·nal [adjective] From Greek *pater* ("father")— having
fatherly feelings
Definition: Having fatherly feelings; having the characteristic of a
father
Usage:
He had ***paternal*** feelings toward his nieces and nephews, since he had no children of his own.
The president addressed the nation in a very ***paternal*** way, since he was the father-figure of the country.
Famous Quotation:

"I felt old and *paternal*. I have ties in my closet older than people in that audience." – Tony Danza, American actor
Related word:
paternalistic [adjective] Acting like a father

339. peer [noun/person, adjective, verb] From Anglo-French *peir* ("equal")— someone of equal rank or status; to look
Definition: To have equal standing with others; also, to look carefully
Usage as a noun:
Once he became a member of the exclusive club, the other members regarded him as a *peer*.
The U.S. Constitution says someone accused of a crime should be tried by a jury of his/her *peers*.
Many students feel some pressure to dress and talk the same way as their *peers*.
Usage as an adjective:
There was a lot of *peer* pressure to use certain language.
Famous Quotation:
"Hermits have no *peer* pressure." – Steven Wright, American actor and writer
Usage as a verb:
She *peered* through the window, and tried to see who was inside the house.

340. per cap·i·ta [adjective] From Latin *per* ("per" – "for each") + *capita* ("head")— per person
Definition: Per person
Usage:
The **per capita** income of people in the United States in 2008 was $39,791.
Because of various economic conditions, countries have different *per capita* incomes.
Famous Quotation:
"The communist nations measure *per capita* poverty, instead of *per capita* income." – Professor Charles

Match the word with the letter of the correct definition.

_____ parochial   (a) someone of equal status

_____ passionate   (b) having a small mind

_____ paternal   (c) having deep feelings

_____ peer   (d) per person

_____ per capita   (e) fatherly

Fill in the blank with the best word. Each word will only be used once.

parochial   passionate   paternal   peer   per capita

(a)   The actors in the play were very _____ in their performances.

(b)   Alice did not understand some of the ideas in the play, because she was from a small town and was _____ .

(c)   People from small towns have a _____ income less than people who live in a city.

(d)   The actors on stage were all working together as

_____ .

(e)   The manager of the theater showed a _____ attitude toward the actors, as if they were his children.

341. per·me·ate [verb] From Latin *per* ("through") + *meare* ("to pass")— to flow easily

Definition: To spread or flow easily and widely

Usage:

The water ***permeated*** the stones and made the entire basement wet.

His knowledge of history ***permeates*** his lectures.

The fear of crime has ***permeated*** the entire society.

Famous Quotation:

"Our thinking is ***permeated*** by our historical myths."— Freeman J. Dyson, English-American mathematician and physicist

342. per·se·ver·ance [noun] From Latin *perseverare* ("to continue severely')— continuing without stopping

Definition: Continuing steadily on a course of action

Usage:

Success is achieved by ***perseverance***, and never giving up.

Although he was tired, he knew that only by continued ***perseverance*** would he be able to get to the top of the mountain before nightfall.

Famous Quotation:

"**Perseverance** is failing 19 times and succeeding the 20th." – Julie Andrews, British actress

Related word:

persevere [verb] To continue without stopping

343. per·sist [verb] From Latin *persistere* ("continue without stopping")— to hold firmly to your stated purpose

Definition: To go to your stated purpose, and to ignore any obstacles

Usage:

He ***persisted*** with his plans, even though many people told him it was not a good idea.

She knew that to become a good dancer she would have to ***persist*** every day.

Famous Quotation:

"That which we *persist* in doing becomes easier for us to do… because our power to do is increased." – Ralph Waldo Emerson, American philosopher and author

<u>Related word</u>:

persistence [noun] Continuing without stopping

344. per·spec·tive [noun] From Latin *per ("through") specere* ("to look at")— a view from a certain position

<u>Definition</u>: A point of view from a different position

<u>Usage</u>:

Everyone who saw the traffic accident had a different *perspective*.

People from different countries often look at things from a different *perspective*.

Since he had travelled to many countries, he had a global **perspective**.

<u>Famous Quotation</u>:

"Everything we hear is a *perspective*, not a truth." – Marcus Aurelius, Roman emperor and philosopher

345. phan·tom [noun] From Latin *phantasma* ("an apparition")— something seen or felt, but having no physical reality

<u>Definition</u>: An unreal appearance; a ghost

<u>Usage</u>:

He believed that all of the ancient gods and deities were *phantoms*.

An artist can paint a *phantom*, and a ghost, even if one does not exist.

<u>Famous Quotation</u>:

"Art has a double face, or expression and illusion: the reality of error and the *phantom* of truth." – Publilius Syrus, Roman author from Syria

Match the word with the letter of the correct definition.

_____ permeate   (a) to stick to your purpose

_____ perseverance   (b) a point of view

_____ persist   (c) a ghost

_____ perspective   (d) to continue without stopping

_____ phantom   (e) to spread

Fill in the blank with the best word. Each word will only be used once.

permeate   perseverance   persist   perspective   phantom

(a)   From the _____ on top of the mountain, the people below looked very small.

(b)   Laurie said she would _____ until she reached the top of the mountain.

(c)   Her colleagues applauded her _____ .

(d)   As they came closer to the top, a feeling of joy _____ the entire group.

(e)   When they reached the summit of the mountain, one of the clouds looked like a _____ in the sky which ancient people described.

346. phil·an·thro·pist [noun/person] From Greek philo ("loving")
+ *anthropos* ("mankind")—someone who loves people

<u>Definition</u>: Someone who helps people

<u>Usage</u>:

After he made a fortune, the man decided to become a ***philanthropist***
and help people.

The ***philanthropist*** gave much of his money to different charities.

<u>Related words</u>:

philanthropic [adjective] Helping people

philanthropy [noun] The effort to help people

<u>Famous Quotation</u>:

"**Philanthropy** simply means love of what it means to be human." –
Valaida Fullwood, American writer

347. phi·los·o·phy [noun] From Greek *philo* ("loving") + *sophia*
("wisdom")— loving wisdom.

<u>Definition</u>: The study of thoughts and wisdom

<u>Usage</u>:

He studied ***philosophy*** in college, in order to learn how to think.

It was the ***philosophy*** of science which interested him the most, to
understand what scientists think, and why.

<u>Famous Quotation</u>:

"***Philosophy*** is a kind of journey, ever learning yet never arriving at the
ideal perfection of truth." – Albert Pike, American military officer

<u>Related words</u>:

philosophize [verb] To think seriously about something

philosopher [noun/person] Someone who thinks carefully about ideas

348. pho·net·ics [noun] From Greek *phonein* ("to make a
sound")— sounds of speech

<u>Definition</u>: The study of words, sounds, and phrases

<u>Usage</u>:

The actors practiced ***phonetics***, in order to pronounce words with the
proper accent in the movie.

Listening to *phonetics* helps actors, teachers, and police determine different dialects.

Famous Quotation:

"**Phonetics** made rapid progress and even came to occupy the central place in the scientific study of language." – Roman Jakobson, Russian-American linguist

Related word:

phonogram [noun] A symbol, or letter, representing a sound

349. pho·to·syn·the·sis [noun] From Greek *photo* ("light") + *synthesis* ("composition" - "putting things together")— the process of combining heat and energy

Definition: Sunlight creating oxygen from plants

Usage:

The oxygen in today's atmosphere is the result of *photosynthesis*, the process by which green plants use the energy of sunlight and synthesize carbohydrates from carbon dioxide and water to create oxygen.

When plants absorb the light of the sun, and create oxygen, the process is called *photosynthesis*.

Famous Quotation:

"We cannot get around *photosynthesis*. All these tiny mechanisms provide the preconditions of our planetary life." – Dame Barbara Ward, British economist and author

Related word:

photosynthesize [verb] To convert into oxygen

350. phys·i·cal [adjective] From Latin *physica* ("the study of nature")— related to the body

Definition: Concerning the body, and not the mind

Usage:

It takes a large *physical* effort to become good in sports.

Physical endurance often requires mental endurance.

Famous Quotations:

"*Physical* fitness is not only one of the most important keys to a healthy body; it is also the basis of dynamic and creative intellectual activity." – John F. Kennedy, American president

"It is curious that *physical* courage should be so common in the world and moral courage so rare." – Mark Twain, American author

Related word:

physics [noun] The study of matter and energy, *physical* things

Match the word with the letter of the correct definition.

_____ philanthropist   (a) pursuit of wisdom

_____ philosophy   (b) related to the body

_____ phonetics   (c) sunlight creating oxygen

_____ photosynthesis   (d) someone who helps people

_____ physical   (e) the sounds of speech

Fill in the blank with the best word. Each word will only be used once.

philanthropist   philosophy   phonetics   photosynthesis   physical

(a)   Larry was very strong, so he loved _____ activity.

(b)   Larry's intellectual curiosity and constant thinking led him to the study of _____ .

(c)   Because Larry wanted to help people, he planned to become a _____ .

(d)   To improve his speaking style, Larry spent time in the study of _____ .

(e)   Scientists learn more every day about how the sunlight works in _____.

Why We Say: *Pipe Dreams*

Pleasant dreams which people had when they smoked opium through a long pipe.

351. pi·ous [adjective] From Latin *pius* "(dutiful"- "devout")—
devoted to religion

Definition: Having religious reverence

Usage:

The priest was very *pious*, praying every morning and every evening.
The church was filled with *pious* people, showing their religious
devotion.

Famous Quotation:

"Some things are better understood by *pious* meditation than by
human language." – Martin Chemnitz, German theologian

Related word:

piety [noun] The quality of being devoted to prayers

Usage as a noun:

"Although we love both the truth and our friends, **piety** requires us to
honor truth above our friends." – Aristotle, ancient Greek philosopher

352. pi·ra·cy [noun] From Latin *pirata* ("see robber)— robbery
committed on the ocean

Definition: Violent robbery on the ocean; now it also pertains to
stealing music or other intellectual property anywhere

Usage:

Most *piracy* occurred before the 20th century, when ships could not
easily defend themselves.

The music business has been a victim of *piracy* for many years, since it
is easy for someone to copy the music and put it on discs to sell.

Famous Quotation:

"I oppose *piracy* and want to see intellectual property protected,
because that is what rewards innovation." – Jared Polis, American
Congressman

Related word:

pirate [noun/person] Someone who commits robbery at sea or steals
intellectual property

353. pla·giar·ize [verb] From Latin *plagiarius* ("a kidnapper of children")— to take someone's creation

Definition: To steal someone else's creations, literary works or ideas.

Usage:

He ***plagiarized*** sentences from someone else's book, and claimed they were his own.

During the political campaign, she ***plagiarized*** the ideas and language of her fellow journalists.

Related Words:

plagiarizer [noun/person] Someone who copies or claim as one's own, the writing or ideas of others.

plagiarism [noun] The act of copying, or claiming as one's own, the writing or ideas of others.

Famous Quotation:

"If we steal thoughts from moderns, it will be cried down as ***plagiarism***; if from the ancients, it will be cried as erudition." – Charles Caleb Colton, English cleric and writer

354. plum·met [verb] From Old French *plomet* ("a ball of lead" dropped in the ocean "to take soundings" to see how deep the ocean is)— something that weighs down or oppresses

Definition: To fall rapidly

Usage:

When he dropped the stone in the ocean, he watched it ***plummet*** toward the bottom.

When he realized that he had failed the test, his optimism began to ***plummet***.

Once the news of the company's problems was made public, the stock price of the company ***plummeted***.

Famous Quotation:

"If you don't climb up the ladder to achieve your goals, your dreams and hopes will ***plummet***." – Professor Charles

355. plunge [verb, noun] From Old French *plongier* ("plunge" or "sink")— to dive

<u>Definition</u>: To dive into something

<u>Usage as a verb</u>:

He ***plunged*** into the water, to save the drowning boy.

She decided to ***plunge*** immediately into the research she had to do.

<u>Famous Quotation</u>:

"***Plunge*** boldly into the thick of life, and seize it where you will, because it is always interesting." – Johann Wolfgang von Goethe, German author

<u>Usage as a noun</u>:

He decided to take the ***plunge***, and get married.

Match the word with the letter of the correct definition.

_____ pious   (a) to fall rapidly

_____ piracy   (b) to dive into something

_____ plagiarist   (c) devoted to prayer

_____ plummet   (d) stealing someone's writing

_____ plunge   (e) robbery at sea

Fill in the blank with the best word. Each word will only be used once.

pious   piracy   plagiarise   plummet   plunge

(a)   Mike was behind schedule, so he decided to _____ into his work.

(b)   Mike was _____ , because he was copying someone else's writing.

(c)   When it was clear that Mike was not honest, his career began to _____.

(d)   By copying someone else's writing Mike was involved in intellectual _____ .

(e)   The priest was _____ , and he prayed for Mike every day.

356. pol·i·cy [noun] From Latin *politia* ("civil administration")— a government plan.

Definition: A plan by a government or by an organization

Usage:

It was the ***policy*** of the U.S. government to provide medical aid to victims of the hurricane.

The company **policy** was that employees had to be at work by 8 o'clock each morning.

Famous Quotation:

"Honesty is the best ***policy***." – Benjamin Franklin, American inventor and statesman

Related words:

politics [noun] Involved in the plans of government

politician [noun/person] Someone involved in the plans of government

police [noun] An official group which administers government laws and policies

357. poll [noun, verb] From Middle German *polle* ("head")— counting the number of heads

Definition: Counting people who are voting or having opinions on something

Usage as a noun:

The politician took a ***poll***, to see how many people were in favor of his ideas.

They took a 'public opinion' ***poll*** to see which candidate would be the best.

Famous Quotation:

"Leadership cannot be measured in a ***poll*** or even in the result of an election. It can only be truly seen with the benefit of time." – Marco Rubio, American Senator

Usage as a verb:

The speaker decided to **poll** the audience to get their opinions.

358. por·tray [verb] From Old French *portraire* ("to paint")— to create a picture

Definition: To create a picture of someone or something

Usage:

She wanted to **portray** her children as intelligent, well-mannered young people.

It was difficult to **portray** the politician, since he had so many different parts of his personality.

Famous Quotation:

"If I am not confident that I can **portray** the character perfectly on the screen, I won't even try." – Meryl Streep, American actress

Related word:

portrayal [noun] The act of creating an image of someone

359. po·tent [adjective] From Latin *potere* ("to be powerful")— having inner power

Definition: Having inner power or influence

Usage:

It was a **potent** chemical, which could cause severe damage.

To achieve great things, love and energy are a **potent** mixture.

To achieve success, knowledge and ambition are a **potent** combination.

Famous Quotation:

"What force is more **potent** than love?" – Igor Stravinsky, Russian composer and musician

Related words:

potential [adjective] Capable of becoming someone or something powerful

potentate [noun/person] Someone who has the power to rule over other people

360. prec·e·dent [noun] From Latin *praecedere* ("to go before")— something that happened earlier

Definition: Something which can be used as an example to follow

There is usually a ***precedent*** for one's actions, since most things were done by someone before.

Most common law is built on ***precedent***, a previous decision on the same subject by earlier judges.

Famous Quotation:

"I have an almost complete disregard for ***precedent***, and a faith in the possibility of something better." – Clara Barton, nurse and founder of the American Red Cross

Related word:

precede [verb] To happen earlier in time

Usage as a verb:

Some music **preceded** the speeches.

Match the word with the letter of the correct definition.

_____ policy   (a) counting people with opinions

_____ poll   (b) to create a picture

_____ portray   (c) having power

_____ potent   (d) something that happened before

_____ precedent   (e) a plan of action

Fill in the blank with the best word. Each word will only be used once.

policy   poll   portray   potent   precedent

(a)   William was now examining the _____ of the government.

(b)   He did not want to create a bad _____ by making the wrong decision.

(c)   As a chemical engineer, William knows how to handle _____ explosives.

(d)   Before making the decision, William took a _____ to see what others thought.

(e)   William wants the press to _____ him as a cautious man.

361. pre·dic·a·ment [noun] From Medieval Latin *prae ("before")* + *dicare ("proclaim")*— something proclaimed as unusual
Definition: An unusual situation, usually an unpleasant one
Usage:
She had a ***predicament***, since her car had a flat tire and she did not know how to fix it.
She was in a strange ***predicament***, having two men who wanted to marry her.
Famous Quotation:
"What makes us human … is to have a smile on our face although we are in a ***predicament***." – Paranjay Malkan, Indian author

362. prej·u·dice [noun] From Latin *prae ("before")* + *iudicium ("judgment")*— a judgment before having any information
Definition: An adverse or unpleasant opinion, formed before having any facts
Usage:
Sometimes it's difficult for people to be free from ***prejudice***.
The judges of the contest had a ***prejudice*** in favor of the girl who was so beautiful.
Some kinds of ***prejudice*** are against a person, and other kinds are in favor of someone.
Famous Quotation:
"***Prejudices***, it is well known, are most difficult to eradicate from the heart whose soil has never been fertilized by education: they grow there, firm as weeds among stones." – Charlotte Bronte, English author
Related word:
prejudicial [adjective] Biased, either harmful or favorable to someone
Usage as adjective:
The journalists were expelled from the event, because their previous statements were ***prejudicial*** to some of those who were participating.

363. pre·scrip·tion [noun] From Latin *prae* ("before") + *scribere* ("to write")— a set of rules

Definition: A set of rules or directions

Usage:

The doctor gave the woman a written **prescription** for some medicine for her sickness.

Refusing to study is a **prescription** for future failure.

Famous Quotation:

"It's a **prescription** for disaster… sooner or later this combustible mixture of ignorance and power is going to blow up in our faces." – Carl Sagan, American astronomer, cosmologist, biologist, and author

Related word:

prescribe [verb] To provide a set of directions

364. pres·tige [noun]   From Latin *praestigium* ("an illusion")— a high level of approval from other people

Definition: Praise and approval given from other people

Usage:

When Marie Curie was the first woman to receive a Nobel Prize, she obtained **prestige** from fellow scientists around the world.

J. K. Rowling obtained international **prestige** when she wrote the *Harry Potter* books.

Famous Quotation:

"Fame is part of me. But the bottom line for me is not **prestige** and power, but having an exciting and creative life." – Matt Dillon, American actor

Related word:

prestigious [adjective] Having respect or approval from others

365. pre·tend [verb] From Latin *pre* ("before") + *tendere* ("to put")— to put a false impression for people to see

Definition: To give a false appearance of yourself

Usage:

To be polite, he **pretended** that he liked the taste of the food.

She had to *pretend* that she enjoyed the concert, but she really did not like the music.

Famous Quotation:

"We are often what we *pretend* to be; therefore, we must be careful about what we *pretend* to be." – Kurt Vonnegut, American author

Related words:

pretense [noun]

Usage: She maintained the **pretense** of enjoying opera.

pretension [noun] The act of creating a false claim

Usage: He continued his **pretensions** of being wealthy, even though he was bankrupt.

Usage as a noun:

People could see that he had many **pretensions**, and that he wanted everyone to think he was smart.

_____ predicament	(a) a level of respect
_____ prejudice	(b) an unpleasant situation
_____ prescription	(c) a bad opinion without information
_____ prestige	(d) to give a false impression
_____ pretend	(e) creating a set of rules

Fill in the blank with the best word. Each word will only be used once.

predicament   prejudice   prescription   prestige   pretend

(a)   Susan had a _____ in favor of the football team from her home town.

(b)   This caused a _____ , because her husband was supporting the other team.

(c)   Her husband's team had more _____ because they were state champions.

(d)   Supporting different teams was a _____ for an argument.

(e)   So, Susan _____ that she did not care which team won the game.

Professor Charles Explains
Why We Say: *Piss Poor*

Originally urine was used to tan animal hides. If the only way a family could earn a living was to collect their urine in a pot and sell it, they were called "***piss poor***."

366. pre·vail [verb] From Latin *pre* ("before") + *valere* ("to have power")— to be greater in strength or influence

Definition: To have power and influence over other people

Usage:

The country with the larger army usually ***prevails*** in a war.

Even though it may take a long time, eventually justice ***prevails*** over injustice.

Famous Quotation:

"Truth will ultimately ***prevail***, where there are pains to bring it to light." – George Washington, first president of the United States

Related words:

prevailing [adjective] Happening most of the time

prevalent [adjective] Happening often

367. priv·i·lege [noun] From Latin *privus* ("private") + *legis* ("law")— a private law for those in power

Definition: A special benefit for certain people

Usage:

The successful students earned the ***privilege*** of meeting the famous actors on stage.

It was a ***privilege*** to meet the Queen of England.

Wealthy people often get special ***privileges***.

Famous Quotation:

"The love of family and friends is much more important than wealth and ***privilege***." – Charles Kuralt, American journalist

Related word:

privileged [adjective] Receiving special treatment

368. pro·ce·dure [noun] From Latin *pro* ("forward") + *cedere* ("to go")— a way of going forward

Definition: A method of doing something

Usage:

The ***procedure*** in a court room is for the judge to make the final decisions.

Removing the tonsils from the body is a standard medical ***procedure***.
The parliament established ***procedures***, so that public issues were
handled in an effective way.

Famous Quotation:

"One test of the correctness of educational ***procedure*** is the happiness
of the child." – Maria Montessori, Italian teacher and founder of the
Montessori Schools

Related words:

proceed [verb] To go forward

process [noun] A series of steps to do something

369. pro·cras·ti·nate [verb] From Latin *pro* ("forward") +
crastinus ("tomorrow")— to put forward until tomorrow.

Definition: To deliberately delay, postpone, or vacillate

Usage:

He never did anything on time, because he would always
procrastinate.

To ***procrastinate*** means to delay until tomorrow something that
should have been done already.

Related words:

procrastinator [noun/person] Someone who constantly delays doing
things

procrastination [noun] The act of delaying

Famous Quotation:

"***Procrastination*** is the thief of time." – Edward Young, English poet
and author

370. prog·no·sis [noun] Latin/Greek *pro* ("before") + *gignoskein*
("come to know")— the probable course of a disease or a series of
events

Definition: A prediction of the probable direction of a disease, or of a
series of events

Usage:

The doctor's ***prognosis*** was that the patient would get well.

The **prognosis** of the economist was disturbing, since it predicted more unemployment.

Famous Quotation:

"I feel great, because the **prognosis** is excellent." – Steven Cojocaru, Canadian television fashion critic

Related Words:

prognosticate [verb] To predict something based upon what you know now

prognosticator [noun/person] Someone who predicts the future based upon present information

Match the word with the letter of the correct definition.

_____ prevail   (a) a special advantage

_____ privilege   (b) to deliberately delay

_____ procedure   (c) to predict a course of action

_____ procrastinate   (d) a way of going forward

_____ prognosis   (e) to have greater power

Fill in the blank with the best word. Each word will only be used once.

prevail   privilege   procedure   procrastinate   prognosis

(a)   It was a _____ for Anne to be able to work with such an important astronomer.

(b)   Anne watched, as the astronomer explained to her the _____ they would use to analyze the stars.

(c)   Anne's friend was supposed to come with her; but he _____ ,and so Anne came without him.

(d)   The astronomer was developing a _____ to explain the trail of the comet.

(e)   The astronomer was careful, and was sure his theories would _____ over the theories of other astronomers.

371. pro·lif·er·a·tion [noun] From Latin *proles ("offspring") + ferre* ("to carry")— growing at a rapid rate

Definition: Growing or spreading rapidly

Usage:

The ***proliferation*** of nuclear weapons around the world is dangerous. The government attempted to stop the ***proliferation*** of misleading information.

Famous Quotation:

"The danger of terrorists and rogue states is compounded by the ***proliferation*** of chemical, biological, radiological, and nuclear weapons." – United Nations Report.

Related word:

proliferate [verb] To spread something rapidly

372. pro·mote [verb] From Latin *promotus* ("moving forward")— to bring attention

Definition: To bring attention to something or someone; to raise to a higher level

Usage:

Apple spent several million dollars to ***promote*** its new iPhone.
The politician gave a speech to ***promote*** his campaign for public office.
The Board of Directors decided to ***promote*** her to the rank of vice president of the company.

Famous Quotation:

"The American position is very clear: we ***promote*** democracy." Ronald Reagan, American president

Related word:

promotion [noun] The act of bringing attention to someone or something; also, receiving a higher position

373. pro·por·tion [noun] From Latin phrase *pro* ("for") + *partio* ("a division")— a part

Definition: A part of something, in relation to a whole

Usage:

The school gave a large *proportion* of the food to the children who had not eaten all day.

While there is still sunlight, the largest *proportion* of the work will have to be done.

Famous Quotation:

"The results you achieve will be in direct *proportion* to the effort you apply." – Denis Waitley, American writer and motivational speaker

Related word:

proportional [adjective] Properly related in size

Usage as an adjective:

Any punishment should be **proportional** to the nature of the crime.

374. pro·pri·e·tor [noun/person] From Medieval Latin *proprietarius* ("owner of property")— an owner.

Definition: Someone who has a legal title to something

Usage:

The *proprietor* decided to close his store early today.

It's the responsibility of the *proprietor* to establish what the working hours are each day.

Famous Quotation:

"We are each the *proprietor* of our own soul." – Professor Charles

Related word:

proprietary [adjective] To have the right of ownership

375. pros·per [verb] From Latin *pro spere* ("from hope")— to succeed

Definition: To be successful, especially financially

Usage:

Because he had worked so hard, his business finally began to *prosper*.

It's very difficult to *prosper* without effort.

Famous Quotation:

"No race can *prosper* until it learns that there is as much dignity in plowing a field as in writing a poem." – Booker T. Washington, American scientist and educator

Related word:

prosperity [noun] The result of becoming successful

Match the word with the letter of the correct definition.

_____ proliferation   (a) spreading rapidly

_____ promote   (b) a part of something

_____ proportion   (c) an owner

_____ proprietor   (d) to be fortunate

_____ prosper   (e) to raise to a higher level

Fill in the blank with the best word. Each word will only be used once.

proliferation   promote   proportion   proprietor   prosper

(a)   The number of magazines available was out of
_____ to the number of people in the city who
would read them.

(b)   There was a _____ of cheap magazines around
the world.

(c)   The company decided to _____ its expensive
magazine by advertising it.

(d)   However, the _____ of the store could not
make money trying to sell it.

(e)   If he tried to sell such an expensive magazine, his business
would not _____ .

376. pro·to·type [noun] From Greek *proto* ("first") + *typos* ("form")— an original form.

Definition: An original type which serves as a model for future production

Usage:

Ford Motor Company developed a ***prototype*** of its new car.

Before producing many items, it's important to actually build a ***prototype*** and test it.

Famous Quotation:

"I love taking an idea... to a ***prototype***, and then to a product that millions of people can use." – Susan Wojcicki, American technology executive

377. pro·trude [verb] From Latin *pro* ("forward") + *trudere* ("to push")— to push out

Definition: To stick out

Usage:

She looked at his large stomach ***protrude*** from his body.

He did not want to ***protrude***, and interrupt the people in the middle of their conversation.

Famous Quotation:

"A good friend can never ***protrude***, because he or she is always welcome." – Professor Charles

Related word:

protrusion [noun] Something which sticks out

378. prox·im·i·ty [noun] From Latin *proximitas* ("nearness")— nearby.

Definition: The state of being nearby

Usage:

When you are in a bus, you are in close ***proximity*** to other people.

People can communicate with others by email, without being in close ***proximity*** to them.

Famous Quotation:

"The moon, by her comparative *proximity*... has always occupied a considerable share of the attention of the inhabitants of earth." – Jules Verne, French author
Related word:
proximate [adjective] Nearby

379. psy·chic [adjective, noun/person] From Greek *psykhikos* ("soul, spirit, mind")—being able to understand or see things before others can
Definition: Capable of extraordinary mental abilities; someone with extraordinary mental powers
Usage as an adjective:
She must be *psychic*, in order to predict who would win the contest. Because she knows what people are going to say, people think she is *psychic.*
Usage as a noun:
Because he can predict so many things in advance, people regard him as a *psychic.*
Famous Quotation:
"Here's something to think about: how come you never see a headline like '*Psychic* Wins Lottery'?" – Jay Leno, American television personality
Related words:
psychiatry [noun] The branch of medicine which deals with the diagnosis, treatment and prevention of mental disorders.
psychiatrist [noun/person] The doctor who helps with mental problems
psychosis [noun] A severe mental disorder
psychotic [adjective] Having a severe mental disorder
psychopath [noun/person] Someone with a severe mental disorder, who is inclined to violence or criminal behavior
psychosomatic [adjective] Greek *psykhikos* ("soul, spirit, mind") + *somatikos* ("the body")— A mental disorder which has physical symptoms

380. qual·i·ty [noun] From Old French *qualité* ("nature")— part of your nature.

<u>Definition</u>: A natural characteristic inside of someone or something

<u>Usage</u>:

He has a strong *quality* of courage, and people think he was born with it.

Her mother told her to always develop her female **qualities**.

The Rolls Royce automobile is very expensive, because its *quality* is very good.

<u>Famous Quotation</u>:

"*Quality* is not an act. It is a habit." – Aristotle, ancient Greek philosopher

<u>Related word</u>:

qualitative [adjective] Relating to the characteristic of someone or something

_____ prototype   (a) nearby

_____ protrude   (b) to see things in advance

_____ proximity   (c) a natural characteristic

_____ psychic   (d) an original model

_____ quality   (e) to stick out

Fill in the blank with the best word. Each word will only be used once.

prototype   protrude   proximity   psychic   quality

(a)   With her close _____ to their neighbors, Mary even shared the aroma from the flowers in their garden.

(b)   The neighbor's garden _____ into Mary's yard.

(c)   The _____ of flowers was excellent, since they were watered daily.

(d)   One of the neighbor boys developed a small
_____ for a new garden tool.

(e)   That boy was so intelligent that some people thought he was
_____ .

Judges in British courts trditionally wore wool wigs. Lawyers could "**pull the wool**" (wig) slightly over his eyes so he could not see something happening.

381. quan·da·ry [noun] From Latin *quando* ("when?")— a state of being unsure.

Definition: A state of uncertainty

Usage:

The parents are in a *quandary*, of where to send their children to school.

She was in a *quandary*, since she did not have a proper dress for the dance.

Famous Quotation:

"A moral *quandary* is usually more difficult to solve than a physical one."— Professor Charles

382. rad·i·cal [adjective, noun/person] From Late Latin *radicalis* ("having roots")— going to the root of something.

Definition: (adjective) Going to the root; (noun/person) a person doing something extreme

Usage as an adjective:

There was a *radical* error in his thesis, since he ignored some basic historical facts.

Albert Einstein had *radical* scientific ideas which changed the entire course of science.

Usage as a noun:

He became a political *radical*, and he turned toward violence.

Famous Quotation:

"Some ideas, once regarded as *radical*, are eventually regarded as common." – Professor Charles

383. rank [noun] From Old French *ranc* ("row" or "line")— a position in an organization

Definition: A position in an organization; an official position

Usage:

He had a very low *rank* in the organization, because he had only joined it recently.

He was working hard to achieve a higher *rank* in the army.

"Success isn't measured by money or power or **rank**. Success is measured by your discipline and inner peace." – Mike Ditka, American football coach

384. rate [noun, verb] From Old French *rate* ("the value")— a measurement
Definition: A method of measurement
Usage as a noun:
He was driving his car at a very high **rate** of speed.
The interest **rate** at the bank to borrow money was very low.
Usage as a verb:
She decided to **rate** the performance very high, since all of the musicians did a good job.
Famous Quotation:
"I don't care to **rate** myself; others can do that." – Felix Baumgartner, Austrian skydiver

385. ra·tio [noun] From Latin *ratio* ("calculating")— a relation in number to other things
Definition: A relationship in degree - or in number - to other things
Usage:
The **ratio** of talented artists, compared to other people in a country, is very small.
It's difficult to calculate the **ratio** of hard-working people, compared to those who don't work.
Famous Quotation:
"Population, when unchecked, increases in a geometric **ratio**." – Thomas Malthus, English scholar and author

Match the word with the letter of the correct definition.

_____ quandary	(a) extreme
_____ radical	(b) a method of measurement
_____ rank	(c) state of uncertainty
_____ rate	(d) relation in number to other things
_____ ratio	(e) a position in an organization

Fill in the blank with the best word. Each word will only be used once.

quandary   radical   rank   rate   ratio

(a)   Mary Leone had a _____ new business idea she wanted to test.

(b)   The business idea could produce a high _____ of return on an investment.

(c)   The idea was based on the _____ of men to women who watch television.

(d)   Mary Leone was confused and in a _____ , because she did not know what to do.

(e)   If her idea were successful, she would be promoted to a higher _____ in the company.

275

386. re·bel [verb, noun/person] From Latin *re* ("again") + *bellare* ("to wage war")— to fight against someone.

Definition: (verb) To reject existing authority; (noun/person) someone who rejects authority

Usage as a verb:

She decided to *rebel* against what was being taught to her, because she disagreed with the ideas.

He *rebelled* against all authority, and eventually he got into trouble.

Usage as a noun:

During the American Civil War, the soldiers of the South were regarded as *rebels*.

The young man was a *rebel*, since he was opposed to the government. The British philosopher and Noble Laureate, Bertrand Russell, was an intellectual *rebel*, since his ideas were different than the ideas of most people at the time.

Famous Quotations:

"To me a *rebel* isn't just someone who breaks the law, but someone who goes against the odds." – William Petersen, American actor and producer

Related word:

rebellion [noun] When many people refuse existing authority at the same time

387. re·cede [verb] From Latin *re* ("back") + *cedere* ("to go")— to slowly move back

Definition: To slowly move back or away

Usage:

When the hair on a man's head starts to *recede* from his forehead, he becomes bald.

When the soldiers were tired, they *receded* from the battle lines.

As informed students displayed their knowledge, the others *receded* from the discussion.

Famous Quotation:

"A single breaker may *recede*, but the tide is coming in." – Thomas Macaulay, British historian and author

Related word:
recession [noun] The act of withdrawing

388. re·cip·i·ent [noun/person] From Latin *recipere* ("to receive")— someone who receives
Definition: A person who receives something
Usage:
After his automobile accident, he was the ***recipient*** of a blood donation.
For her brain research, Mary-Britt Moser was the ***recipient*** of the Nobel Prize in 2014.
Aleksandr Solzhenitsyn was the ***recipient*** of the Noble Prize for Literature in 1970.
Famous Quotation:
"It is better to be the **recipient** of your own self-respect, then of someone else's praise." – Professor Charles

389. re·ci·pro·cate [verb] From Latin *recus* ("backward") + *procus* ("forward")— to go back and forth.
Definition: To give back in an equal way
Usage:
He gave Christmas gifts to his neighbors, to ***reciprocate*** for the gifts they had given him.
She wanted to ***reciprocate*** for all of the things her teacher had taught her.
Famous Quotation:
"Take time to appreciate your employees, and they will ***reciprocate*** in a thousand ways." – Ben Nelson, American Senator
Related word:
reciprocity [noun] The act of returning benefits and help to others

390. re·con·cil·i·a·tion [noun] From Latin *re ("again") + concilare* ("make friendly")— the act of becoming friendly again
Definition: Re-establishing or renewing a relationship

Usage:

After years of war, the countries began the process of ***reconciliation***.

Although they were both angry, they decided the time had come for ***reconciliation***.

Famous Quotation:

"If there is to be ***reconciliation***, first there must be truth." – Timothy B. Tyson, American author and historian

Related word:

reconcile [verb] To settle or re-establish a relationship

Match the word with the letter of the correct definition.

_____ rebel	(a) someone who receives
_____ recede	(b) to return benefits or help
_____ recipient	(c) re-establishing a relationship
_____ reciprocate	(d) to refuse authority
_____ reconciliatio	(e) to slowly move away

Fill in the blank with the best word. Each word will only be used once.

rebel   recede   recipient   reciprocate   reconciliation

(a)   Daniel was the _____ of an award for his successful management skills.

(b)   Many employees wanted to _____ for his help to them.

(c)   Everyone knew Daniel was a _____ , who always did things differently.

(d)   He always did his best and would never _____ into the background.

(e)   Daniel also helped employees who had disagreements to make a _____ .

391. rec·ti·fy [verb] From Old French *rectifier* ("to make straight")— to make straight
Definition: To make right, or to correct
Usage:
She had to *rectify* the errors which the students made.
It was important to *rectify* the errors on the document.
Famous Quotation:
"The reason I keep making movies is I hate the last thing I did. I'm trying to *rectify* my wrongs."—Joaquin Phoenix, American actor

392. re·form [verb] From Latin *reformare* ("to form again")— to improve
Definition: To improve by correcting errors
Usage:
The college president wanted to *reform* the entire curriculum of the school.
The principal of the school decided to *reform* the policies of how the students should dress.
Famous Quotation:
"Each generation doubtless feels called upon to *reform* the world." – Albert Camus, French journalist and author
Related word:
reformation [noun] The result of something being improved

393. reg·u·late [verb] From Latin *regulare* ("to rule by restrictions")— to make rules
Definition: To control by making rules and laws
Usage:
The manager decided to *regulate* the number of employees who could work on weekends.
The principal of the school had to *regulate* the hours when athletes could use the gymnasium.
Famous Quotation:

"A wise and frugal government, which shall restrain men from injuring one another, shall leave them otherwise free to *regulate* their own pursuits." – Thomas Jefferson, American president and scholar

Related words:

regulations [noun] Rules put into place to control people

regular [adjective] Ordinary (rules for guidance)

394. rel·ic [noun] From Old French *relique* ("the body part or other object from a holy person")— something from the past that has survived

Definition: Something from the past that has survived

Usage:

It was a *relic* from a saint who died many centuries ago.

His old ideas were like *relics* from the past.

Famous Quotation:

"It is very difficult to hang onto the **relics** of history." – Iris Chang, American journalist

395. rep·re·sent [verb] From Latin *re* ("again") + *praesentare* ("to show" or "to present")— to stand in place of someone or something.

Definition: To stand in the place of someone; to symbolize something

Usage:

The lawyer *represented* the man in court, and spoke on behalf of him.

The art museum had several paintings which *represented* the styles of different artists.

The Irish flag *represents* the country of Ireland.

Famous Quotation:

"The aim of art is not to *represent* the outward appearance of things, but their inner significance." – Aristotle, ancient Greek philosopher

Related word:

representative [noun/person] Someone who speaks for another person or a group

Match the word with the letter of the correct definition.

_____ rectify   (a) to improve by changing
_____ reform   (b) something from the past
_____ regulate   (c) to stand in place of someone
_____ relic   (d) to correct
_____ represent   (e) to control by making rules

Fill in the blank with the best word. Each word will only be used once.

rectify   reform   regulate   relic   represent

(a)   As the new president, Nate wanted to _____ the entire company.

(b)   Nate created new rules to _____ the employees more carefully.

(c)   There were many mistakes which he would have to _____ .

(d)   Some of the old technology in the company was a _____ of the past.

(e)   The employees chose someone to _____ them in the meetings with Nate.

Professor Charles Explains
Why We Say: *Read between the lines*

For centuries, secret messages were written 'between the lines' of a letter, using milk or lemon juice. Recipients could heat the letter to **"read between the lines."**

282

396. res·er·voir [noun] From Old French *reserver* ("to reserve"), and French *réservoir* ("a storehouse")— a natural or artificial lake to store water

Definition: A place to store water

Usage:

Fort Peck Dam, on the Missouri River, is a major ***reservoir*** in the United States.

Lac de Serre-Poncon in the Provence Region of France, built across the Durance River, is one of the largest ***reservoirs*** in Europe and is a hydro-electric power station.

He had a ***reservoir*** of ideas that he had been accumulating for many years.

Famous Quotation:

"Music is a ***reservoir*** … of sounds." – Dexter Gordon, American musician

Related word:

reserve [verb, noun] To save something for later

Usage as a verb:

They had to **reserve** the tickets for the theater last night.

Usage as a noun:

"Love is a sacred **reserve** of energy; it is like the blood of spiritual evolution." – Pierre Teilhard de Chardin, French paleontologist and author

397. re·sid·u·al [adjective, noun] From Latin *re* ("back") + *sedere* ("to sit")— sitting back

Definition: Remaining behind or left over

Usage as an adjective:

After the rain stopped, there was **residual** water on the roads.

When their relationship ended, they both had ***residual*** feelings.

Famous Quotation:

"We are challenging … seeking contradictions or small, persistent ***residual*** errors." – Carl Sagan, American astronomer, cosmologist, biologist, and author

Usage as a noun:

When singers create an album, there are continued payments made to them over the years called '*residuals*.'

Related words:

reside [verb] To remain or live in a place

398. re·sign [verb] From Old French *resigner* ("renounce")— to quit

Definition: To give up, or accept as inevitable

Usage:

He decided to **resign** from his important position.

She **resigned** from her job.

She was **resigned** to the fact that she could not afford a new car.

Famous Quotation:

"To **resign** from efforts to improve ourselves is to **resign** from living." – Professor Charles

Related word:

resignation [noun] The act of resigning

399. re·sist [verb] From Latin *re ("against") + sistere* ("to stand")— to remain firm against

Definition: To remain firm against, or to fend off some attack

Usage:

She decided to **resist** the demands of those who wanted more money.

He **resisted** the temptation to have another glass of wine.

Famous Quotation:

"Life is a series of natural and spontaneous changes. Don't **resist** them – that only creates sorrow. Let things flow naturally forward." – Lao Tzu, Chinese philosopher

Related word:

resistance [noun] The act of opposing something

400. re·sume [verb, noun] From Latin *re* ("again") + *sumere* ("to take up")—to begin again

Definition: To begin again; to start over

Usage as a verb:

As soon as the car was repaired, they were able to *resume* their trip.

After he paused to take a breath, he *resumed* his speech.

Famous Quotation:

"I want to *resume* the life of a shy person." – Garrison Keillor, American author and TV personality

Usage as a noun:

He prepared his *resumé* in order to look for a new job.

Match the word with the letter of the correct definition.

_____ reservoir	(a) to quit
_____ residual	(b) to oppose
_____ resign	(c) a place to store water
_____ resist	(d) remaining behind
_____ resume	(e) continue

Fill in the blank with the best word. Each word will only be used once.

reservoir   residual   resign   resist   resume

(a)   The power of the water was so strong that the
_____ could no longer hold it.

(b)   After the flood, there was only a _____ amount of water left.

(c)   Mayor Watson had to _____ because he had not prepared the town for a flood.

(d)   Mayor Watson could not _____ the demands of the people for him to quit.

(e)   After the flood, the people in the town began to
_____ their lives.

401. re·tain [verb]   From Latin *retinere* ("to hold back")— to hold back

Definition: To keep

Usage:

The store had to advertise every day in order to *retain* its customers.

He worked hard to *retain* his reputation as an interesting professor.

Famous Quotation:

"In the end we *retain* from our studies only that which we practically apply." – Johann Wolfgang von Goethe, German author

402. re·trieve [verb] From Old French *re* ("again") + *trouver* ("to find")— to get back

Definition: To get back; to save

Usage:

The family looked everywhere to *retrieve* their lost dog.

The student had to *retrieve* the lost data on her computer.

Famous Quotation:

"I never could *retrieve* a dream." – Theodore Sturgeon, American science fiction author

Related word:

retrieval [noun] The act of getting something back

403. re·volve [verb] From Latin *re* ("again") + *volvere* ("to roll")— to roll around a central point

Definition: To go around a fixed point

Usage:

The earth *revolves* around the sun every 365.256 days, called a sidereal year.

Their troubles always seem to *revolve* around money, and how much money they need.

For him, everything *revolves* around the book he is writing.

Famous Quotation:

"I am only in contact with things that *revolve* around love." – Marc Chagall, Russian-French artist

Related word:
revolving [noun] Happening again and again

404. re·ward [noun, verb] From Anglo-French *reward*
("repayment" – for some service)— something given for good behavior
Definition: Something given for good behavior, or for finding
something or someone
Usage as a noun:
He received a *reward* for finding the lost dog.
The police offered a *reward* for anyone who gave information to find
the criminal.
Famous Quotation:
"The highest *reward* for a person's effort is not what they get for it,
but what they become by it." – John Ruskin, English author
Usage as a verb:
For their hard work, the teacher *rewarded* her students by giving them
new laptops.

405. ri·gor [noun] From Old French *rigor* ("strength")— strictness or
firmness
Definition: Hard; firm
Usage:
He pursued the matter with a *rigor*, because he wanted to succeed.
Mathematics requires a continued *rigor*, and a constant attention to
detail.
Famous Quotation:
"We need more *rigor* in all kinds of programs." – Margaret Spellings,
American educator
Related word:
rigorous [adjective] Hard or difficult
Usage as an adjective:
To be successful you must often have a **rigorous** work schedule.

Match the word with the letter of the correct definition.

_____ retain   (a) strictness
_____ retrieve   (b) something given for good behavior
_____ revolve   (c) to get back
_____ reward   (d) to keep
_____ rigor   (e) to roll around

Fill in the blank with the best word. Each word will only be used once.

retain   retrieve   revolved   reward   rigor

(a)   Lucy offered a large _____ for finding the lost cat.

(b)   When they found the cat, Lucy went to _____ it.

(c)   Lucy was happy, because her life _____ around that cat.

(d)   Lucy's daily chore and _____ was to take care of the cat.

(e)   Lucy was trying to _____ her reputation for taking care of cats.

406. rite/rit·u·al [nouns] From Latin *ritus* ("religious observance")— a religious procedure

Definition: A religious ceremony; a regular religious practice

Usage:

Religious *rites* and *rituals* have been going on for thousands of years.

Some *rituals* do not concern religion, for example the *ritual* of appointing a new president.

For some people, watching their favorite television program every week is a *ritual*.

Famous Quotation:

"*Ritual* is important to us as human beings. It ties us to our traditions and our histories." – Miller Williams, American poet and author

Related word:

ritualistic [adjective] Concerning a procedure for doing things

407. ros·ter [noun] From Dutch *rooster* ("table list")— a list

Definition: A list, usually of names

Usage:

The coach added the names of the new athletes to the *roster* of those on the football team.

Several students added their names to the *roster* of those who are seeking scholarships.

Her name was on the *roster* of candidates who wanted to be president.

Famous Quotation:

"The most important *roster* is the list of good people in your life." – Professor Charles

408. ro·tate [verb] From Latin *rotare* ("turning around in a circle")— to go in a circle

Definition: To spin in a circle around a center point (an axis)

Usage:

The earth *rotates* every day, for a period of 24 hours with respect to the sun, which is why there is a change from daylight to darkness.

The army sergeant *rotated* his troops, so that each of them had a turn performing night duty.

Related word:

rotation [noun] The act of going around in a circle

Famous Quotation:

"I shall now call to mind that the motion of the heavenly bodies is circular, since the motion appropriate to a sphere is **rotation** in a circle." – Nicolaus Copernicus, Prussian- Polish astronomer, who discovered that the sun is the center of the universe, and not the sun. [The earth itself *rotates* in a circle, but the planet earth revolves around the sun.]

409. sac·ri·fice [noun, verb] From Latin *sacra* ("sacred" or "holy") + *facere* ("to do" or "to perform")— offering a gift to a deity

Definition: A gift to a deity; to give up something for a greater good

Usage as a noun:

For thousands of years, people have offered *sacrifices* to their gods.

It is often necessary to make a *sacrifice*, in order to achieve some form of greatness.

Parents have to make *sacrifices*, to take care of their children.

Usage as a verb:

Many people *sacrifice* their lives, to help others.

Famous Quotation:

"To give anything less than your best is to *sacrifice* your gift." – Steve Prefontaine, American Olympic athlete

410. safe·guard [noun, verb] From Middle French *sauve* ("safe") + *garde* ("keep")— a protection

Definition: A protective device, either a mechanical device or a legal device

Usage as a noun:

The high fence was a *safeguard* against any wild animals coming on to his property.

The lawyer added a clause to the contract, as a *safeguard* against future fraud.

Usage as a verb:

The family put up a fence, to *safeguard* their children from dogs.

He found it necessary to *safeguard* his property.

Famous Quotation:

"Don't interfere with anything in the Constitution. That must be maintained, for it is the only *safeguard* of our liberties." — Abraham Lincoln, American President

Match the word with the letter of the correct definition.

_____	rite/ritual	(a) a list
_____	roster	(b) to go in a circle
_____	rotate	(c) to give up something
_____	sacrifice	(d) someone providing protection
_____	safeguard	(e) a religious procedure

Fill in the blank with the best word. Each word will only be used once.

rite/ritual   roster   rotate   sacrifice   safeguard

(a)   It was a big _____ for Jack to give up football in order to pursue his studies.

(b)   Jack is on top of the academic _____ , and needs to study to remain there.

(c)   It's important to _____ his status on that list.

(d)   Jack has to _____ his class schedule in order to get the courses he needs.

(e)   Studying has now become a daily _____, just like a religious program.

Why We Say: *Stool Pigeon*

To attract pigeons, hunters would tie a pigeon to a stool; its cry of alarm would attract other pigeons. Thus, the **"stool pigeon"** was regarded as a squealing traitor.

411. sa·ga [noun] Old Norse *saga* ("story")— a long story

Definition: A long story, usually written down

Usage:

The father told his son about the old, Icelandic *saga* of sailing the ocean.

The kings of Norway and Norse Vikings created many *sagas* about their travels.

Famous Quotation:

"The *sagas* of history tell us how people lived in ancient times, before we arrived." – Professor Charles

412. scan·dal [noun] From Late Latin *scandalum* ("cause for offense") — a publicized incident about something offensive to society

Definition: Something bad and inappropriate which is made public

Usage:

The politician was involved in a major bribery *scandal*, in which he took money for his vote.

When the actress divorced her husband, it became a **scandal**.

Famous Quotation:

"Previously, you had to be famous to afford *scandals*, but now you need a *scandal* to become famous." – Maurice Chevalier, French Actor

413. scar [noun, verb] From Old French *escare* ("scab formed after a burn")— a mark left on the skin after an injury

Definition: A permanent mark left after some act

Usage as a noun:

The burn on his hand left a large *scar*, which he had for his entire life.

The pain of her husband's death left a *scar* on her heart.

Famous Quotation:

"*Scars* remind us where we have been. They don't have to dictate where we are going." – Joe Mantegna, American Actor

Usage as a verb:

His bad behavior *scarred* his reputation for life, since no one would ever forget what he did.

414. sec·u·lar [noun] From Latin *saecularis* ("not belonging to any religious group")—not spiritual or religious

Definition: Worldly, rather than spiritual

Usage:

It was a *secular* society, and it did not have many religious people in it.

Science has *secular* theories, and not religious ones.

Ironically, the *secular* laws in the United States protect against religious discrimination.

Famous Quotation:

"As far as the public is concerned, India is amazingly *secular*." – Shah Rukh Khan, Indian actor and producer

415. seize [verb] From Old French *seisir* ("to take possession by force")— to grab by force

Definition: To grab suddenly and with force

Usage:

The leaders of ancient Rome used their military force to *seize* the neighboring lands.

The Spanish conquistadors *seized* the gold from the Americas and took it back to Spain.

Famous Quotation:

"Progress occurs when courageous, skillful leaders *seize* the opportunity to change things for the better." – Harry S. Truman, American president

Related word:

seizure [noun] The act of taking something by force; also, something taken by force

Match the word with the letter of the correct definition.

_____ saga   (a) a mark from an injury

_____ scandal   (b) to grab by force

_____ scar   (c) a long story

_____ secular   (d) a bad act

_____ seize   (e) not religious

Fill in the blank with the best word. Each word will only be used once.

saga   scandal   scar   secular   seize

(a)   The politician was involved in a bribery _____ .

(b)   The politician's bad behavior left a _____ on his reputation.

(c)   His opponent could now _____ the opportunity to win.

(d)   Both the religious community and the _____ community now supported the politician's opponent.

(e)   The newspaper stories were now becoming a long _____ .

416. sen·ti·ment [noun] From Latin *sentire* ("to feel")— a feeling

Definition: An attitude or feeling, toward someone or something

Usage:

He told people of his affectionate *sentiments* for her.

The American *sentiment* is a feeling for the importance of freedom.

Famous Quotation:

"Public *sentiment* is everything. With public *sentiment*, nothing can fail. Without it, nothing can succeed." – Abraham Lincoln, American president

Related words:

sentimentality [noun] Having feelings

sentimental [adjective] Expressing feelings toward someone or something.

Usage as an adjective:

When he returned to the house of his childhood, he became very **sentimental** and started to cry.

417. Sep·tem·ber [noun]

Usage:

On *September* 25, 1888 the first transfusion of human blood was performed at Guy's Hospital in London.

September 8th is the International Literacy Day!

Famous Quotation:

"I'll see you in *September*, when the moon is blue…"— Song

Related words:

septuagenarian [noun/person] A person who is 70-79 years old

418. se·quence [noun] From Latin *sequens* ("to follow")— one thing following another

Definition: A following of one thing after another, in succession

Usage:

Mathematics is a logical *sequence*, since one step follows another.

To assemble a piece of machinery, there is a *sequence* of simple steps in which one part must be installed and then the next.

It was a strange *sequence* of events, which eventually led to the war.

Famous Quotation:

"Our lives are a *sequence* of things. When we are alive, they are continuing." – Simon McBurney, English director and actor

Related word:

sequential [adjective] When things happen one after the other

419. se·vere [adjective] From Latin *severus* ("very serious")— harsh

Definition: Harsh and strict; extremely serious

Usage:

He had a *severe* wound on his leg from the car accident.

He received *severe* punishment for his bad behavior.

Famous Quotation:

"Every human being must find his own way to cope with *severe* loss." – Caleb Carr, American military historian

Related word:

severity [noun] Something very serious

Usage as a noun:

The **severity** of the loss of their father was hard for the children to overcome.

420. shame [noun] From Old English *scamu* ("feeling of guilt")— feeling guilty

Definition: Feeling bad, because you did something wrong; a disappointment

Usage:

When he was caught stealing, his parents felt a sense of *shame*.

It was a *shame* that she failed the examination.

Famous Quotation:

"Being ignorant is not so much a *shame*, as being unwilling to learn." – Benjamin Franklin, American inventor and statesman

Related word:

ashamed [adjective] Feeling bad for doing something wrong

Famous Events in September: *Sept. 16, 1620: the small ship (c.113 ft x 25 ft)* **Mayflower** *left England for a two-month voyage to America with 102 passengers and a crew of 30.*

September wasn't always the ninth month, you know.

September was once the 'seventh' (*septem* in Latin) month in the old Roman calendar

Match the word with the letter of the correct definition.

_____ sentiment   (a) extremely serious
_____ September   (b) ninth month of the year
_____ sequence   (c) feeling bad for doing wrong
_____ severe   (d) a feeling
_____ shame   (e) one thing following another

Fill in the blank with the best word. Each word will only be used once.

sentiment   September   sequence   severe   shame

(a)   The weather was wonderful in _____ , so there was a large crowd of people for the game.

(b)   There was an unfortunate _____ of events which led to the problems.

(c)   The pitcher on the baseball team had a _____ injury to his arm.

(d)   It was a _____ that the pitcher could not attend.

(e)   The _____ of the crowd was disappointment.

421. shrink [verb] From Old English *scrinan* ("to make smaller")—
to make smaller
Definition: To make smaller
Usage:
The woman decided to ***shrink*** some of her daughter's dresses, because
they were too large for her.
When you dry your clothes with heat, they may ***shrink***.
When it is your time to act, you should never ***shrink*** from your
responsibilities.
Famous Quotation:
"The massive bulk of the earth ***shrinks*** to insignificance when
compared to the size of the heavens." – Nicolaus Copernicus, Prussian-
Polish astronomer
Another use of the word:
shrink [noun/person] A humorous name for a psychiatrist because the
psychiatrist '***shrinks***' your mental problems.

422. shut·tle [noun, verb] From Old English *scytel* ("to throw a
dart")— a 14th century weaving instrument with the 'dart' (needle)
going travel back and forth to create cloth
Definition: To move back and forth over a short distance
Usage as verb:
The astronauts had to ***shuttle*** back and forth, a two day trip between
earth and the International Space Station.
The school bus had to ***shuttle*** the children to school and home every
day.
Usage as noun:
The original ***shuttle*** was a tool used to hold yarn in order to make
clothing.
One big problem in the space program is the cost of building the space
shuttle.
Famous Quotation:
"I slept while floating in the middle of the flight deck, the upper deck of
the space ***shuttle***." – Sally Ride, American astronaut

423. sib·ling [noun/person] From Proto-Germanic *sibja* ("a blood relative")—close relative
Definition: Individuals having one or both parents in common
Usage:
She had five *siblings*, three brothers and two sisters.
He regretted that he did not have any *siblings*, since he was all alone.
Famous Quotation:
"Friends are the *siblings* which God never gave us." – Mencius, Chinese philosopher

424. sig·nif·i·cant [adjective] From Latin *signum* ("sign") + *facere* ("to make")— to make important
Definition: Something meaningful or important
Usage:
The end of World War II was a *significant* event.
It was *significant* that she did not tell him the entire story.
The fact that he was an hour late for the meeting was very *significant*.
She was his *significant* 'other.'
Famous Quotation:
"The *significant* problems we face cannot be solved at the same level of thinking we were at when we created them." – Albert Einstein, American scientist
Related words:
significance [noun] The importance of something
signify [verb] To point out or denote something important

425. sim·u·late [verb] From Latin *simulare* ("to make similar")— to imitate
Definition: To imitate, or to create a substitute
Usage:
To *simulate* the weightlessness of space, the astronauts train in a chamber without air.
Actors and actresses have to *simulate* what the real people would do in the same situation.

"There is no disguise which can hide love for long where it exists, or *simulate* love when it does not exist." – Francois de La Rochefoucauld, French author

Related words:

simulation [noun] The condition of imitating something

Usage as a noun:

The astronauts were in a weightless room, which was a **simulation** of how it would feel to walk in space.

similar [adjective] Having the same looks

Usage as adjective:

The two boys look **similar,** because they have the same size and hair color.

Match the word with the letter of the correct definition.

_____ shrink   (a) a brother or sister

_____ shuttle   (b) to imitate

_____ sibling   (c) to make smaller

_____ significant   (d) to travel back and forth

_____ simulate   (e) important

Fill in the blank with the best word. Each word will only be used once.

shrink   shuttle   sibling   significant   simulate

(a)   Daniel's brother was his only _____ .

(b)   Daniel loved to _____ his little brother back and forth to school.

(c)   Daniel's brother was a _____ part of his life.

(d)   Daniel would never _____ from doing things for his brother.

(e)   There was no way to _____ the happiness he had when he was with his brother.

426. sin·cere [adjective] *Sine* (without) + *cera* (wax). (In ancient Rome dishonest stone dealers often hid a marble's imperfections with wax. Then a law required all stones to be *sine* (without) + *cera* (wax), 'without wax' – "sincere")— genuine

Definition: Genuine; real

Usage:

He was *sincere*, when he expressed his affection for his friends.

She told her daughter how *sincere* he was, in wanting to provide things for her.

Famous Quotation:

"The *sincere* friends of this world are as ship lights in the stormiest of nights." – Giotto di Bondone, Italian painter and architect

Related word:

sincerity [noun] The quality of being honest or genuine, and having no falsehood or deceit

427. sin·is·ter [adjective] From Latin *sinister* ("on the left" or "left hand")— using the left hand

Definition: Something threatening evil

Usage:

 He looked at them with a *sinister* smile.

The criminal had *sinister* intentions.

Famous Quotation:

"When a *sinister* person intends to become your enemy, they begin by trying to become your friend." –   William Blake, English poet and painter

428. smug·gle [verb] From Dutch *smokkelen* ("to transport things illegally")— to avoid customs duties

Definition: To import or export something illegally, without paying customs duties

Usage:

They *smuggled* diamonds across the border, to avoid paying customs duties.

He was caught, when he tried to *smuggle* drugs across the border.

Famous Quotation:

"To *smuggle* is one of the oldest criminal activities in human history."
– Professor Charles

Related word:

smuggler [noun/person] Someone who imports or exports without paying customs duties

429. so·lar [adjective] From Latin *solaris* ("the sun")— pertaining to the sun

Definition: Something regarding the sun

Usage:

She wanted to use *solar* energy for her entire house.

They have a *solar* heating system in their building, with *solar* panels on the roof.

When the moon covers the sun, we have a *solar* eclipse, and we cannot see the sun.

Famous Quotation:

"The *solar* system should be viewed as our back yard." – Neil deGrasse Tyson, American astrophysicist, scientist, and author

Related word:

solarium [noun] Room with windows to let in the sun

430. sole [adjective, noun] From Latin *solus* ("alone")— alone

Definition: Alone

Usage as an adjective:

She is the *sole* living member of the entire family, since the others all died.

His job at the factory was his *sole* source of income, since he had no other money.

Famous Quotation:

"Your *sole* contribution to the sum of things is yourself." – Robert Crandall, American businessman and former president of American Airlines

Other meanings – as a noun:

(1) *sole*: The bottom of your foot; (2) **sole**: The flat part of the bottom of your shoe; (3) **sole**: A variety of fish

Usage as a noun:

When he stepped on some glass, it cut the **sole** of his shoe, and hurt the **sole** of his foot.

He liked fish and wanted to have some filet of **sole** for dinner, with a glass of white wine.

Match the word with the letter of the correct definition.

_____ sincere   (a) to import or export illegally

_____ sinister   (b) concerning the sun

_____ smuggle   (c) alone

_____ solar   (d) genuine

_____ sole   (e) bad or evil

Fill in the blank with the best word. Each word will only be used once.

sincere   sinister   smuggle   solar   sole

(a) Igor wanted to _____ diamonds out of Russia.

(b) His _____ purpose was to make money.

(c) His friends gave me _____ advice, for him to stop his crimes.

(d) He had a very _____ plot, because he did not care about the law.

(e) He hid the diamonds in the _____ panels on the roof of the house.

Professor Charles Explains
Why We Say: *Sinister*

Someone or something which is wicked, nefarious, or iniquitous. From Latin *sinister* ("on the left" or "left hand")

431. sol·id [adjective]   From Latin *solidus* ("firm")— firm and strong
<u>Definition</u>: Firm and strong, not made of gas or liquid
<u>Usage</u>:
The building was a ***solid*** structure, since it was made of stone.
Their relationship was ***solid***, because they had been friends for a long time.
<u>Famous Quotation</u>:
"Humility is the ***solid*** foundation of all virtues." – Confucius, Chinese philosopher
<u>Related words</u>:
solidarity [noun] A strong union of members of a group
solidify [verb] To make solid.
<u>Usage as a verb</u>:
In order to trust each other, they had to **solidify** their relationship.

432. source [noun] From Old French *sourse* ("to rise")— the beginning place
<u>Definition</u>:   The point at which something begins
<u>Usage</u>:
The river from the mountain was the ***source*** of the water that flowed into the lake.
The organic food he ate was the ***source*** of his good health.
<u>Famous Quotation</u>:
"Silence is a ***source*** of great strength." – Lao Tsu, Chinese philosopher

433. spec·trum [noun] From Latin *spectrum* ("appearance")— the appearance of light from the distribution of energy
<u>Definition</u>:   The distribution of light, or energy, or ideas and people
<u>Usage</u>:
The sky was lit up with an unusual ***spectrum*** of lights.
The teacher was pleased to see that her students had a whole ***spectrum*** of ideas from their studies.
<u>Famous Quotation</u>:

"Literature … keeps you aware of a wider *spectrum* of human activities." – Abraham Verghese, American medical professor and author

Related words:

spectacle [noun] Something that can be seen, usually a public event

spectacular [adjective] Describing a very impressive sight or event

Usage as an adjective:

The circus was a **spectacular** event, which everyone in the audience enjoyed.

434. spin·ster [noun, person] (A female spinner of thread in the 1660s in the English textile mills who worked long hours and was unable to marry.)— an unmarried woman

Definition: An unmarried woman.

Usage:

 She was still a *spinster*, even when she was 50 years old.

A *spinster* has more time for a career, since she has no responsibilities for a family.

Famous Quotation:

"A *spinster* has different opportunities for self-fulfillment than a married lady."— Professor Charles

435. sta·bil·i·ty [noun]   From Latin *stabulum* ("standing room" or "stable") (Originally, a solid and secure building to protect animals) — firmness, reliability, or steadfastness.

Definition: Firm, reliable, and resistant to change.

Usage:

The *stability* of the parents leads to constructive lives of the children.

Despite the emotional pressures of his responsibilities, the president maintains his *stability*.

If the scientist does not control the *stability* of the chemicals, they may explode.

Famous Quotation:

"Law is the essential foundation of *stability* and order, both within societies and in international relations." – J. William Fulbright, American politician and educator

Related Words:

stable [adjective]   The quality of being solid and secure

Match the word with the letter of the correct definition.

_____ solid   (a) unmarried woman

_____ source   (b) firm and reliable

_____ spectrum   (c) firm

_____ spinster   (d) a variety of things or people

_____ stability   (e) place where something begins

Fill in the blank with the best word. Each word will only be used once.

solid   source   spectrum   spinster   stability

(a)   Because Linda was a _____ , she had time to work many hours.

(b)   Linda created another _____ of income to earn money.

(c)   Linda had a large _____ of business activities.

(d)   Linda's new opportunity was very _____, because there was no risk.

(e)   Financial _____ was Linda's main concern.

Professor Charles Explains
Why We Say: *Spinster*

Would the lady care to join me for a spring picnic?

Sure. My next day off is in February.

CARTER

An unmarried woman. From the Latin *spinnen* ("spin") + *stere* (female suffix). In the Middle Ages a female spinner of thread in the English textile mills worked long hours and was unable to marry.

436. sta·tus quo [noun] From Latin *status("state")* + *quo ("in which)*— the present state of things

Definition: The present state of affairs; things as they are now

Usage:

He wanted to maintain the ***status quo***, since he was afraid of change.

Those who are in power usually prefer to keep the ***status quo***, to keep their power.

All progress comes from not accepting the ***status quo***.

Famous Quotation:

"Everyone that has ever done anything significant first found themselves in the place where the ***status quo*** was no longer enough."
– Temit Ope Ibrahim, American writer

437. stig·ma·tize [verb] From Greek *stigmatizein* ("to blemish" or "to get dirty")— to harm someone's name or reputation

Definition: To mark someone as bad

Usage:

The politician tried to ***stigmatize*** his opponent, by making false accusations about him.

Because of his background, the man was unfairly ***stigmatized***.

Famous Quotation:

"Scientists are often ***stigmatized*** for disclosing the new facts which destroy ancient beliefs." – Professor Charles

438. strat·e·gy [noun] From French *stratégie* ("art of a general")— a plan to win

Definition: The art and science of using all abilities and resources to win

Usage:

The generals developed a military ***strategy*** to win the war.

The football coach needed a different ***strategy*** to beat the competition.

Famous Quotation:

"The only *strategy* that is guaranteed to fail is not taking risks." – Mark Zuckerberg, American founder of Facebook
Related word:
strategize [verb] To develop a plan
strategic [adjective] Well-planned

439. struc·ture [noun]   From Latin *structura* ("a building")— something built or assembled
Definition: Something constructed from a number of parts held together
Usage:
The *structure* of the school building was built with steel and stone.
The writer developed an unusual *structure* for his new novel.
Famous Quotation:
"If you come from a solid family *structure*, it doesn't matter what you go through in your life. You're going to be okay." – Alyssa Milano, American actress
Related word:
structural [adjective] Relating to something built or assembled
Usage as an adjective:
The building was constructed with **structural** steel.

440. sub·si·dize [verb] From Old French *subside* ("to make a contribution")— to provide financial assistance
Definition: To provide financial assistance
Usage:
The government decided to *subsidize* the schools, in order to hire more teachers.
The orchestra was *subsidized*, by donations from the public.
Famous Quotation:
"When you *subsidize* poverty and failure, you get more of both." – James Dale Davidson, American financial manager
Related word:
subsidy [noun] Money given to someone or to an organization

Match the word with the letter of the correct definition.

_____ *status quo*   (a) a plan to succeed
_____ stigmatize   (b) something built
_____ strategy   (c) to provide financial help
_____ structure   (d) present state of affairs
_____ subsidize   (e) to call someone bad

Fill in the blank with the best word. Each word will only be used once.

status quo   stigmatize   strategy   structure   subsidize

(a)   Nat was not satisfied with the _____ , and wanted to do something new.

(b)   Nat developed a simple _____ to create a new charity.

(c)   To do it, Nat had to put a financial _____ in place.

(d)   He wanted wealthy people to _____ his efforts with whatever money they were willing to give.

(e)   He would not _____ people, even if they did not help him.

441. sub·tle [adjective] From Latin *subtilis* ("thin" or "delicate")—
small and difficult to detect

Definition: Difficult to see or detect; elusive

Usage:

She gave him a ***subtle*** smile, and he did not know what that meant.

Some people have ***subtle*** minds, because they don't reveal everything
they are thinking.

There is a ***subtle*** difference between the two shades of blue, because
they are almost the same.

Famous Quotation:

"If you have an important point to make, don't try to be ***subtle*** or
clever." – Winston Churchill, British Prime Minister and author

Related word:

subtlety [noun] Something small and difficult to understand

442. sur·veil·lance [noun] From French *surveillance*
("oversight")— observation

Definition: Close observation of someone or a group, especially
someone under suspicion

Usage:

The police kept the suspicious man under ***surveillance***, to watch where
he went every day.

For general protection, cameras are placed in public places to keep
crowds under ***surveillance***.

Famous Quotation:

"Everybody calls everyone a spy, secretly, in Russia, and everyone is
under ***surveillance***. You never feel safe." – Agnes Smedley, American
journalist and writer

Related word:

surveil [verb] To keep under close observation

443. sur·vive [verb] From Latin *super* ("over") + *vivere* ("to live")—
to live longer

Definition: To remain alive

Usage:

When the Titanic hit an iceberg, many people did not *survive*.

When they were lost in the mountains, they only had a small amount of food to help them *survive*.

The author's ideas may not *survive* the criticism and analysis of so many people.

Famous Quotation:

"Love and compassion are necessities, not luxuries, and without them humanity cannot *survive*." – Dalai Lama, Religious leader of Tibetan Buddhism

Related word:

survival [noun] The act of staying alive

444. sus·pect [verb, noun/person] From Latin *suspectare* ("to look with distrust")— to assume something, without proof

Definition: (verb) To believe that something may be true, without proof; (noun/person) a person who is believed to have done something wrong

Usage as a verb:

The mother *suspected* that the dog ate her new cake.

The teacher *suspected* one of her students for writing the words on the wall.

Famous Quotation:

"The old believe everything, the middle-aged *suspect* everything, the young know everything." – Oscar Wilde, Irish playwright and author

Usage as a noun/person:

The police captured the man and arrested him as a **suspect** in the robbery.

Related words:

suspicious [adjective] Something which looks like it may be true

suspicions [noun] Reasons for thinking something may be true

445. sus·pend [verb] From Latin *suspendere* ("to hang up")— to hold

Definition: To hold up or delay

Usage:

The man was **suspended** from the bridge by a long rope.

The baseball game was **suspended** because of the rain.

The college football player was **suspended** from the team, because he did not get good grades.

Famous Quotation:

"Most people **suspend** their judgment, until someone else has expressed theirs, and then they repeat it." – Ernest Dimnet, French priest and author

Related words:

suspension [noun] The act of being delayed for a period of time

suspenders [noun] Elastic straps that hold up trousers

Match the word with the letter of the correct definition.

_____ subtle   (a) to stay alive

_____ surveillance   (b) to delay for a while

_____ survive   (c) a possible criminal

_____ suspect   (d) close observation

_____ suspend   (e) small and hard to see

Fill in the blank with the best word. Each word will only be used once.

subtle   surveillance   survive   suspect   suspend

(a)   The police _____ Peter of hitting someone.

(b)   The police kept Peter under _____ day and night.

(c)   The police could not _____ their investigation until they had the evidence.

(d)   The doctors hoped the victim of the assault would _____ the attack.

(e)   When talking to reporters, the doctors were cautious and very _____.

446. sym·bol [noun] From Greek *symbolon* ("a watchword" or "a representation")—a representation of someone or something

Definition: Something or someone who represents something else

Usage as noun:

The American flag is a *symbol* of the United States of America.

The cross is a *symbol* of Christianity, and the crescent moon is a *symbol* of Islam.

Lady Justice, from the Roman goddess Justice, with a blindfold, scale, and a sword, is a *symbol* of justice.

Famous Quotation:

"Words are just *symbols* for the relation of things to one another and to us."— Friedrich Nietzsche, German philosopher and author

Related words:

symbolic [adjective] Having the quality of representing an idea or country

symbolize [verb] To represent an idea or a country

Usage as verb:

The United Nations **symbolizes** the desire to have a peaceful approach to international events.

447. tan·gi·ble [adjective] From Latin *tangere* ("to touch")— provable by touching.

Definition: Provable by touching it; something you can see or feel

Usage:

There is a *tangible* smoothness to the baby's skin, and you can feel it easily.

Friendship is a *tangible* thing, because you can almost feel it.

Famous Quotation:

"If malice or evil were *tangible* and had a shape, they would be in the shape of a boomerang." – Charley Reese, American journalist and writer

Related word:

tangent [noun] A mathematical term, meaning something touches a line but does not cross it

448. ter·mi·nal [adjective, noun] From Latin *terminus* ("end" or "a boundary")— the end

Definition: The limit

Usage as an adjective:

The man had ***terminal*** heart disease, and he only had six more months to live.

Famous Quotation:

"We're all ***terminal***. None of us is getting out of this alive." – Valerie Harper, American actress

Usage as a noun:

The final stop of the train was at the city ***terminal***.

Related word:

terminate [verb] To end

Usage as a verb:

The company decided to **terminate** the employee, because he was not doing a good job.

The lady didn't want to talk any longer, so she **terminated** the conversation.

449. thresh·old [noun] Old English '*Thresh*' + '*hold*.' [Thresh (straw) covered the dirt or wooden floor of homes and restaurants to absorb spilled food and drink. A piece of wood (the "threshold") was put by the bottom of the door to 'hold' the 'thresh' (straw) in the house when people walked out the door.]— a piece of wood or stone placed by a door

Definition: An entrance or doorway

Usage:

The groom carried the bride over the ***threshold*** of their new home as a married couple.

He walked across the ***threshold*** to greatness.

Famous Quotation:

"It is possible that mankind is on the ***threshold*** of a golden age." – Bertrand Russell, British philosopher and Nobel Laureate

450. tol·er·ate [verb] From Latin *tolerare* ("to bear" or "to withstand")— to allow or permit

Definition: To allow, without prohibiting or stopping it

Usage:

She *tolerated* the noise from the children, because they were having fun.

She could no longer *tolerate* the men smoking in the bus.

Famous Quotation:

"I cannot *tolerate* fools. I only want to associate with brilliant people."
– Ida Lupino, American actress

Related words:

tolerance [noun] The act of not objecting to other people's behavior

tolerant [adjective] Having the quality of not objecting to other people's behavior

Match the word with the letter of the correct definition.

_____ symbol   (a) to allow

_____ tangible   (b) to end

_____ terminate   (c) floor by an entrance door

_____ threshold   (d) a representation

_____ tolerate   (e) to prove by touching

Fill in the blank with the best word. Each word will only be used once.

symbol   tangible   terminate   threshold   tolerate

(a)   Michelle's new clothing designs put her on the
_____ of success.

(b)   Michelle is a hard worker and does not _____
people who don't work hard.

(c)   In the fashion industry, Michelle has become a
_____ for hard work.

(d)   Michelle expects _____ results from the people
who work for her.

(e)   If one of her employees does not do their job, Michelle will
_____ them.

451. trend [noun] From Middle English *trenden* ("to turn around")— a direction in which something moves
Definition: The direction in which something moves
Usage:
The *trend* was for people to watch movies at home, and not in theaters.
The advertising departments of stores create *trends*, in order to obtain customers.
Famous Quotation:
"For me, clothes are like character; I don't follow fashion or understand **trends**." – Meryl Streep, American actress

452. trig·ger [noun, verb] From Dutch *trekken* ("to pull")— the lever on a gun to fire it
Definition: The lever on a gun to fire it; an event which ignites other events
Usage as noun:
The man taught his son to be careful, when his finger is on the *trigger* of the gun.
Usage as verb:
The shot fired from the ship Aurora *triggered* the Russian Revolution.
The sad retirement of their old friend from the company *triggered* a wave of tears.
Famous Quotation:
"The creative process is very mysterious. A conversation, a ride in the car, or a melody can *trigger* something." – Alejandro Gonzalez Inarritu, Mexican film producer and director

453. ul·te·ri·or [adjective] From Latin *ulterior* ("distant" or "remote")— hidden or concealed
Definition: Hidden or concealed, sometimes deliberately in order to deceive
Usage:

Some movie-makers have an *ulterior* reason for making a movie, because they want to send a political message to the audience.

The politician had an *ulterior* motive for helping the women's club, because he wanted their votes.

Famous Quotation:

"We need to be kind, unconditionally and without any *ulterior* motive … even when we don't want to be." – Josh Radnor, American Actor and Screenwriter

454. un·der·stand [verb] To grasp something with your mind

Definition: To mentally comprehend the nature of something

Usage:

I *understand* what I read in the newspaper.

He said he does not *understand* what the politician said.

Related word:

understanding [noun] Comprehending something

Famous Quotation:

"Peace cannot be kept by force; it can only be achieved by *understanding.*" – Albert Einstein, American scientist

455. u·ni·ver·sal [adjective] From Latin *universalis* ("happening everywhere")— being everywhere

Definition: Affecting the entire world, and beyond

Usage:

It's a *universal* truth that all people want to be happy.

Music is a *universal* language which unites people.

Famous Quotation:

"A warm smile is the *universal* language of kindness." – William Arthur Ward, American author

Related word:

universe [noun] The planet earth and all the galaxies and stars.

Professor Charles Explains
Why We Say: *Understand*

To receive guidance, Hammurabi, the king of ancient Babylon, would **'stand under'** the engraved image of the Sun God on a tall stele (pillar) and ask for advice.

Match the word with the letter of the correct definition.

_____ trend   (a) hidden or concealed
_____ trigger   (b) to grasp with your mind
_____ ulterior   (c) being everywhere
_____ understand   (d) the lever of a gun
_____ universal   (e) the direction something goes

Fill in the blank with the best word. Each word will only be used once.

trend   trigger   ulterior   understand   universal

(a)   There is a _____ desire among people around the world to have peace.

(b)   One of the best ways to have peace is for people to _____ each other.

(c)   There is a _____ to try to solve all problems through diplomacy.

(d)   Some politicians have _____ motives for what they tell the public.

(e)   If politicians say the wrong thing, they can _____ a war.

456. u·til·ize [verb] From Latin *utilis* ("useable")— to use

Definition: To use something

Usage:

She was able to *utilize* her education in economics to obtain a good position.

He was in a hurry to *utilize* the new farm equipment, which he had just purchased.

Famous Quotation:

"I love to *utilize* my celebrity status in a responsible and constructive way." – William Baldwin, American actor

Related word:

 utility [noun] The quality of being useful.

457. van·ish [verb] From Latin *evanescere* ("to disappear")— to disappear

Definition: To disappear quickly without a trace

Usage:

The ship *vanished* in the storm, and no one knew if it sunk beneath the sea.

When they found the dog, all of their fears *vanished*.

Famous Quotation:

"It's been my philosophy of life that difficulties *vanish* when they are faced boldly." – Isaac Asimov, American professor of biochemistry and writer

458. van·i·ty [noun] From French *vanite* ("self conceit")— false pride

Definition: False pride about one's looks or accomplishments

Usage:

Her *vanity* is one of the reasons people dislike her.

Many famous people starve their personal happiness, in order to feed their fame and *vanity*.

When people pretend to accept your *vanity*, you are living in a world of illusions.

326

"*Vanity* is a mask of arrogance that tries to hide insecurity." – Professor Charles

459. ver·dict [noun] From Latin *ver* ("truth") +*dire* ("to say")— a true report.

Definition: A decision by a judge or jury after examining the evidence

Usage:

The *verdict* of the jury at the trial was that the man is guilty of the crime.

The jury was unanimous in coming to a final *verdict* in the trial.

Famous Quotation:

"Those who invoke history will be judged by history, and will have to accept history's *verdict*." – Dag Hammarskjold, former Secretary General of the United Nations

460. ver·sus [adverb] From Latin *versus* ("against")— against

Definition: Against, or opposing

Usage:

In the trial, it was the plaintiff *versus* the defendant.

It was Ronald Reagan *versus* Jimmy Carter in the 1980 American presidential election.

In law, it is 'national security surveillance' *versus* the 'invasion of privacy.'

Famous Quotation:

"When it's knowledge *versus* ignorance, education will win … eventually." – Professor Charles

Match the word with the letter of the correct definition.

_____ utilize   (a) to disappear

_____ vanish   (b) a decision

_____ vanity   (c) against

_____ verdict   (d) to use

_____ versus   (e) false pride

Fill in the blank with the best word. Each word will only be used once.

utilize   vanish   vanity   verdict   versus

(a)   It was one lawyer _____ another lawyer in the court room.

(b)   Both lawyers tried to _____ every tactic they could to win.

(c)   The smiles and _____ of the defendant were upsetting to watch.

(d)   When the _____ was read by the jury, the defendant was guilty.

(e)   You could see the smiles _____ from the defendant's face.

461. ves·tige [noun] From Latin *vestigium* ("footprint")— remaining evidence of the past

Definition: A visible trace or sign that something happened in the past

Usage:

There was a ***vestige*** of the ancient civilization, left over in the pottery which was discovered.

A ***vestige*** of a nation's folk lore remains within every society.

Famous Quotation:

"No matter how many lies are told to hide the truth, a ***vestige*** of truth will always remain." – Professor Charles

462. vil·lain [noun/person] from Latin, *villanus* (" A lowly paid farmhand" who worked on a *villa* [a small farm] and would sneak into a town at night to steal or pillage)— a person who does something bad

Definition: A person who does something bad.

Usage:

The police caught the ***villain*** with the things he had stolen.

The ***villains*** came into town to see what they could destroy.

Famous Quotation:

"I like the military. I guess in a world of ***villains*** and heroes, they're my heroes." – John Cena, American wrestler and actor

Related word:

villainous   [adjective] Having the qualities of a bad behavior

villainy [noun] An evil action

463. vi·o·la·tion [noun] From Latin *violare* ("to treat with dishonor")— breaking a law

Definition: Breaking a law or promise

Usage:

Many people have traffic ***violations***, because they drive their cars too fast.

To prevent the woman from participating in the event was a ***violation*** of her civil rights.

For him to speak at the conference is a ***violation*** of their rules.

Famous Quotation:

"To be dishonest is a **violation** of one's own honor."— Professor Charles

Related word:

violate [verb] To cause harm to someone, or to break a law

464. vit·ri·ol·ic [adjective] From Old French *vitriol* ("glass" –when heated, creates an acid) — bitter and abusive

Definition: Bitter and abusive language or expressions

Usage:

Nice language brings people together, but **vitriolic** language makes enemies.

Vitriolic actions of angry people create tensions.

Famous Quotation:

"We will have to repent not merely for the **vitriolic** words of the bad people, but for the appalling silence of the good people." – Martin Luther King, Jr., minister and civil rights leader

Related word:

vitriol [noun] Sulfates of metals; abusive or angry feelings or language

465. voy·age [noun] From Old French *voiage* ("a journey")— a long journey

Definition: A long journey to another land

Usage:

The entire family took an ocean **voyage** around the world.

Life is a **voyage** of discovery and learning.

Famous Quotation:

"The **voyage** of discovery is not in seeking new landscapes, but in having new eyes." – Marcel Proust, French author

Related word:

voyageur [noun/person] A traveler

Professor Charles Explains

Why We Say: *Villain*

A lowly paid farmhand (Latin, *villanus*) who worked on a villa and would sneak into town at night to steal or rape was called a "**villain**."

Match the word with the letter of the correct definition.

_____ vestige   (a) someone who does bad things

_____ villain   (b) breaking a law

_____ violate   (c) ocean journey

_____ vitriolic   (d) remaining evidence of the past

_____ voyage   (e) bitter and abusive

Fill in the blank with the best word. Each word will only be used once.

vestige   villain   violate   vitriolic   voyage

(a)   The purpose of Heath's trip was to search for any
_____ of ancient civilizations.

(b)   The long ocean _____ was full of excitement.

(c)   One of the reasons for excitement was that there was a
_____ on board the ship.

(d)   People who _____ the law on the ocean go to jail.

(e)   When he was caught by the ship police, the language of the
thief was _____.

466. vul·ner·a·ble [adjective] From Latin *vulnerare* ("to hurt")— easily hurt

Definition: Susceptible to injury or attack; easily harmed

Usage:

The castle was **vulnerable** to attacks from the enemy army.

The company is **vulnerable** to cyber attacks from hackers.

She has sensitive feelings, and she is **vulnerable** to being hurt very easily.

Famous Quotation:

"We're never more **vulnerable** than when we trust someone. But, paradoxically, if we cannot trust, neither can we find love or joy." – Walter Anderson, American journalist

467. with·draw [verb] From Old English *wid* ("to back away") + *drawen* ("to draw")— to go back

Definition: To take back or take away

Usage:

The woman had to **withdraw** some money from her bank account.

The general decided to **withdraw** his troops from the battle.

He **withdrew** his name from the contest.

Famous Quotation:

"There is always time to add a word, never to **withdraw** one."— Baltasar Gracian, Spanish Jesuit philosopher

Related word:

withdrawal [noun] Something taken back

468. with·hold [verb] From Old English *wid* ("to back away") + Middle English *holden* ("to hold")— to hold back

Definition: To keep back

Usage:

The father decided to **withhold** any allowance from his son, until his grades improved.

The police agreed to **withhold** the names from the public.

The people at the political rally **withheld** information from the press.

"It's as impossible to **withhold** information from the receptive mind, as it is impossible to force it upon the unreasoning mind." – Agnes Repplier, American writer

469. wit·ness [noun/person, verb] From Old English *witnes* ("someone who has personal knowledge")— someone who has personal knowledge

Definition: Someone who has personally seen or heard something

Usage as a noun:

She was a **witness** to the traffic accident, because she saw both cars collide.

Good journalists are **witnesses** to history, and report the facts for everyone to read.

Famous Quotation:

"The eyes are more exact **witnesses** than the ears." – Heraclitus, Ancient Greek philosopher

Usage as a verb:

She **witnessed** the accident and reported it to the police.

470. wound [noun, verb] From Old English *wund* ("injury")— an injury to the body

Definition: An injury, to the body or to someone's feelings

Usage as a noun:

He had an old **wound** on his leg, from the time he was attacked by a bear in the mountains.

The doctor gave her medicine for the **wound** on her arm.

She felt a deep **wound**, from the things that were said against her.

Famous Quotation:

"A broken bone can heal, but the **wound** a word opens can fester forever." – Jessamyn West, American writer

Usage as a verb:

The rock fell and **wounded** the boy who was walking on the path.

His harsh words **wounded** the spirit of the group.

Match the word with the letter of the correct definition.

_____ vulnerable   (a) an injury

_____ withdraw   (b) to remove something

_____ withhold   (c) someone who has knowledge

_____ witness   (d) easy to be hurt

_____ wound   (e) to hold back

Fill in the blank with the best word. Each word will only be used once.

vulnerable   withdraw   withhold   witness   wound

(a)   The result of the automobile accident created a large _____ on the lady's leg.

(b)   Walter was an important _____ to the accident.

(c)   Walter wanted to _____ from the police interview and go home.

(d)   The police told Walter not to _____ any information about the accident.

(e)   The lawyers knew Walter was _____ because he was weak .

471. xen·o·phile [noun/person] From Greek *xeno* ("foreign") + *philos* ("to love")— a person who loves foreign things and people
Definition: A person likes foreign people, manners, and cultures
Usage:
Since her parents were diplomats, she was a ***xenophile*** all of her life.
He regarded things from foreign countries as exotic, probably because he was a ***xenophile***.
Famous Quotation:
"All educated people are ***xenophiles***, because they appreciate our common bond of humanity." – Professor Charles
Related word:
xenophilia [noun] Love of foreign things and people

472. xen·o·pho·bic [adjective] From Greek *xeno* ("foreign") + *phobia* ("fear")— afraid of foreign things or people
Definition: A person who does not like - or is afraid of - foreign things or people
Usage:
Ignorant people are more ***xenophobic*** than people who are educated.
When a flood of immigrants came into the country, there was a surge of ***xenophobic*** feelings. Related word:
xenophobia [noun]Fear of foreign people or things
Famous Quotation as a noun:
"Time and again we see leaders and members of religions incite aggression, fanaticism, hate, and ***xenophobia***." – Hans Kung, German Catholic theologian

473. yield [verb, noun]   From Old English *gieldan* ("to pay")— to produce, or to surrender
Definition: To be productive; to give up possessions
Usage:
With proper cultivation, the farmer's field can ***yield*** many bushels of corn.
When the country lost the war, they had to ***yield*** much of their land to the victors.

336

The teenager pleaded with his father to use the car, but the father would not *yield*.

<u>Famous Quotation</u>:

"Do not *yield* to misfortunes, but advance more boldly to meet them." – Virgil, Ancient Roman writer

<u>Usage as a noun</u>:

This year the harvest produced a large *yield* of corn.

474. zeal·ous [adjective] From Latin *zelus* ("zeal" or "passion")— filled with energy for a cause

<u>Definition</u>: Motivated by fervor for a particular religion or political cause

<u>Usage</u>:

The religious community was *zealous*, saying their prayers every day.

The football fans were *zealous*, and they cheered every time their team scored a touchdown.

<u>Famous Quotation</u>:

"No one would be more *zealous* than myself to establish effectual barriers against the horrors of religious tyranny, and every species of religious persecution." – George Washington, first president of the United States

<u>Related words</u>:

zeal [noun] Enthusiastic devotion for a cause

zealot [noun/person] A person who has excessive fervor; a fanatic

475. zone [noun] From Latin *zona* ("geographical belt")— an area regarded as separate for some reason

<u>Definition</u>: An area or region which is set aside for a particular purpose

<u>Usage</u>:

The innocent people in the war fled to the safe *zone*, which the United Nations had provided.

The football player ran to the End *Zone* for the touchdown.

Libraries are often regarded as quiet **zones**.

<u>Famous Quotation</u>:

"Life begins at the end of your comfort *zone*." – Neale Donald Walsch, American author

Match the word with the letter of the correct definition.

_____ xenophile	(a) to produce or surrender
_____ xenophobic	(b) enthusiastic devotion
_____ yield	(c) a particular area
_____ zealous	(d) someone who fears foreigners
_____ zone	(e) someone who loves foreigners

Fill in the blank with the best word. Each word will only be used once.

xenophile   xenophobic   yield   zealous   zone

(a)   Cynthia was a happy and _____ traveler.

(b)   Cynthia was a _____ , who loved people from everywhere.

(c)   Being educated, none of the students had ever been
_____ .

(d)   During the ocean voyage, the students changed their watches as they went through each time _____.

(e)   Being so small on such a wide ocean, they realized how ancient people could _____ to fate.

Professor Charles Explains
Why We Say: *Saved by the Bell*

To aid people accidentally buried alive, a bell was put on the outside of coffins with a string inside. If the person awoke, they could pull the string and be "**saved by the bell**."

Professor Charles Says....

Why we say:

1. **AM and PM**   AM is *ante meridiem* in Latin, and means 'before the middle of the day', namely before noon; *post meridiem* in Latin means 'after the middle of the day', after noon … in English 'afternoon.'

2. **a square meal**   In the English Royal Navy under Lord Nelson, to prevent food plates from sliding off the eating bench, pieces of wood were nailed in the shape of a 'square.' So, to have a full meal, without losing any of the food, was called "a square meal."

3. **actions speak louder than words**   This means that people watch what you do, and do not always believe what you say.

4. **Achilles heel (tendon)**   To totally protect the Greek hero Achilles, his mother dipped him into the River Styx. To do so, she held him by the back of his heel (his tendon). Therefore, Achilles' heel was left uncovered and the only part of his body that was not protected. So, someone's "Achilles' heel" is their weak spot.

5. **against the grain**   When using a saw to cut wood, it is more difficult to cut across the grain of the wood than to cut 'with the grain.' So, whoever does things in a difficult way is said to 'go against the grain.'

6. **apartment**   From Roman author Virgil (70BC-19BC) *appartare*, to live apart. Now, it is a private residence which is not a house.

7. **assassin**   *Hashishiyyi*, ("hashish users") An Ismaili Muslim sect in the 11th century, who murdered Sunni Muslims. To further blacken the reputation of these killers for violating the laws of Islam, the term

'assassin' was used by the Sunni Muslims to accuse them of being drugged on hashish, because the use of drugs is forbidden in Islam.

8. **beat around the bush**   Hunters would flush animals or birds out of their hiding places in bushes. To avoid hitting the animal accidentally, they would not hit the bush directly; they would beat around the bush. So, to 'beat around the bush' means to avoid saying something directly.

9. **bedlam**   The St Mary of Bethlehem lunatic asylum, founded in 15th century London, was referred to as 'Bedlem.' Because the patients were loud and difficult to control, 'bedlam' now means a state of noisy uproar and confusion.

10. **bend someone's ear**   To 'bend' someone's outer ear over the auditory canal to keep out noise, so they can hear you better when you whisper.   Now, it usually means telling people some gossip, namely something bad about someone.

11. **beyond the pale**   Throughout history, white (pale) fence posts mark the boundary of a specified area. To go beyond the pale, was to go where you should not go. Later, to say or do something wrong was to go "beyond the pale."

12. **big wig**   In the early 17th century, Louis XIII of France (perhaps because he was prematurely bald) wore a big wig on his head. To imitate him, other men wore big wigs as a fashion statement to show their importance. Now, when people are important, or pretend to be important, they are ridiculed and called a 'big wig.'

13. **blackmail**   In 16th century Scotland, clan chieftains had the unlawful (black) practice of demanding extra rent (mail) from local farmers for 'protection.' Now, blackmail is when someone demands a 'protection' payment from you to keep something about you secret.

14. **Blue Blood**   Because veins are blue, in Medieval times many aristocrats thought their blood was blue, and that common people had red blood. So, 'blue blood' refers to aristocrats.

15. **bone up**   'Bone' was used as a verb 'to study' since the 19th century, probably because bones were used to polish leather to get the shoes and boots ready for wear. Now, 'bone up' means to polish yourself and get prepared.

16. **booze**   Variant of Middle English 'bouse,' an 18th century term for heavy drinking. Now, it means any alcoholic beverage.

17. **bridal bouquet**   Why do brides carry flowers? Centuries ago, after winter was over, most people took their first bath in May. To conceal her odor at weddings, the bride carried a bouquet of flowers. It then became a custom.

18. **bring home the bacon.**   To impress guests with expensive food, the wife would tell husbands "bring home the bacon." Now, it means to get a job and bring home some money.

19. **burning question of the day**   During the Christian Inquisition in Europe in the Middle Ages, heretics were burned alive. So, "the burning question of the day" that fearful believers asked was, 'What heresy did the person commit, to be burned alive?'

20. **bury the hatchet**   Iroquois Indians would bury their weapons of war as a symbol of newly-created peace. Now, to 'bury the hatchet' means to make peace with someone.

21. **by the same token**   Old English *tacuian,* a symbol. It matters how a symbol is used. 'By the same token (symbol)' means someone might conclude something entirely differently – from looking at the same facts.

22. **carry a torch** The Greek god of marriage, *Hymenaios*, carried a torch and lit the fire in the hearth in the wedding home to keep the love fire burning. Now 'to carry a torch' for someone means to have a flame of love in your heart for him or her.

23. *chauffeur* From French *chauffer* (to heat), the *chauffeur* was the man who heated up the early steam-driven cars to get the engine warm. Now, it means someone who is your driver.

24. **chew the fat** Before refrigeration, a host would cut pieces of fat bacon as a snack, and everyone would sit and 'chew the fat' while talking. Now it means to sit around and talk.

25. **coach** In the Hungarian town of *Kocs* in the 1500s, a carriage (*kocsi*) was created. In England in the 18th century, students were 'coached' ("carried") by teachers to help them to their goal of passing the exams. Now, a coach is anyone who gives you advice, and is often associated with sports.

26. **cold feet** One explanation is that a 'fear response' can cause hyperventilation, slowing the blood flow to the extremities, causing 'cold feet' and temporary paralysis. Now it means to be afraid to do something.

27. **cold shoulder** For dinner, house guests who overstayed their welcome were given the worst part of the animal to eat, not warmed up, the 'cold shoulder.' Now it means to be unfriendly to someone.

28. **cost an arm and a leg** Probable origin is World War I where soldiers lost limbs trying to seize a hill. It 'cost an arm and a leg.' Now, if something is expensive, people say 'it cost an arm and a leg.'

29. **could not hold a candle to...** Before electricity, boys were hired to light the way at night for those who could afford to pay them.

Undependable boys 'could not hold a candle to' those people. Now, it means that someone who does not do a good job 'could not hold a candle to' someone does a job better.

30. **cut the red tape**   British solicitors (lawyers) kept their clients' documents in a file folder carefully folded with red ribbons. To retrieve papers they would often have to 'cut the red tape.' Now it means to cut through the delays, and move forward.

31. **dashboard**   Originally a 'board' to protect the driver of a carriage from mud thrown up by the hooves of horses that 'dashed' in front of him. Now, it is the inside of the front of the car.

32. **deadline**   During the U.S. Civil War prisoners were often confined in open areas, with boundary lines. If they crossed the line, they were shot. Now, it means a time by which something must be done, or there will be severe consequences.

33. **dirt poor**   In the past, only the wealthy people could cover their dirt floors with slate or wood. Others were "dirt poor." Now, it means anyone who is very poor.

34. **eat humble pie**   In the 14th century, *umbles* was the name given to the intestines (heart, liver, entrails) of a deer and was made into a pie for the peasants. The Master and upper classes ate better cuts of meat. Now, it means to be reduced in dignity, or to be 'put down' and embarrassed.

35. **face the music**   Most say it comes from military firing squads: a blind-folded person stood, back against a wall, unable to see his executioners, but would 'face the music', usually drums. Now it means to admit what you did wrong.

36. **flash in the pan**   In the 1700s, the 'pan' of a flintlock musket held the gunpowder. If the powder flared up but did not fire a bullet, it

344

was a 'flash in the pan.' It looked good, but it did not perform. Now, a 'flash in the pan' is someone who starts out well, but then quickly burns out.

37. **fly off the handle**   In the 19th century America, if someone swung his axe too violently and hit the target with the handle instead of with the head (the metal part), the head would fly off the handle. So, the expression to describe people who lose control and are violent is that they are 'flying off the handle.'

38. **flying by the seat of his pants**   Early airplanes did not have any instruments to provide the pilots with information. Pilots could only estimate engine problems by the vibrations under their seats.   Now, it means to make decisions when you don't have enough information.

39. **for the birds**   It means something 'worthless.' It stems from pre-automobile times, when birds would eat seeds in the horse droppings on the street. "For the birds" is a polite expression for, "It's manure."

40. **fortnight**   Fourteen nights (*ftowertyne niht*) , the ancient German method of counting by nights. (Some people think it comes from the 'Night Watch' in England, where the guards had to remain at the watch towers on top of a fort for 14 nights, a "fort night," and then their rotation was over for the month.)

41. **go beserk**   Viking warriors were called 'Beserker' because they wore bearskin coats *('berserkr'* or *'bear sark').* They were ferocious fighters, often eating hallucinogenic mushrooms before battles. So, they looked like they were crazy. Now, people who don't act normal are said to 'go bezerk.'

42. **go scot free**   'Scot' is from the ancient Norse word *skot,* a payment due from a tenant to a landlord, or a tax. If it was not paid, the

person went 'scot free.' Today, it means someone who is not convicted of a crime.

43. **going to the clink** Clink Prison was a famous prison in London since the 12th century. Although the prison is no longer there, the Clink Prison Museum and Clink Street remain. Now, 'going to the clink' means going to prison.

44. **Good-bye** 'Good-bye' is a contraction of "God be with you." In many languages it is, "Go with God," namely, *adios* in Spanish, *adieu* in French, etc

45. **Good night. Sleep tight.** In Shakespeare's time, mattresses were 'tightened' on bed frames by ropes to make them firm for a good night's sleep. If the ropes were "tight" the mattress would be flat and not sag down. Now, it means 'Have a nice sleep.'

46. **got up on the wrong side of the bed** An old superstition says that it was bad luck to put your left foot down first when getting out of bed. Now, if someone is in a bad mood, people say that he 'got up on the wrong side of the bed.'

47. **high on the hog** Poor people eat pigs' feet. The tastier parts of the meat are higher on the hog. So, if you eat 'high on the hog,' you are wealthier.

48. **holding a wake** Before modern medicine, people often went into a deep sleep, and looked like they were dead. To avoid people being accidentally buried alive, relatives would "hold a wake" (a party) for two days to see if the corpse would "wake" up from the loud noise.

49. **hotheaded** An expression based on the idea that anger generates additional blood flow to the brain, causing heat, a reddened face, and 'hot headed' irrational behavior.

50. **husband**   From Old Norse (Northern German, Scandinavia), a *husbondi* was the man who managed the farm and the house... and the occupants. Now, a husband is the man in a marriage, and a wife is the woman.

51. **in the limelight**   In the 1820s, Goldsworth Gurney invented an oxy-hydrogen blowpipe and added a piece of 'lime' stone to create a brilliant light to shine on the actors who were on stage. They were then "in the lime light." Now, anyone who becomes famous is 'in the limelight.'

52. **infantry**   From 16th century Italy, the *infanteria* ('infants') were too young or inexperienced to be in the cavalry and manage horses. Now, the infantry are the foot soldiers in the army.

53. **It didn't pan out.**   Prospectors during the American Gold Rush poured water into pans to wash out the gravel and dirt from what they dug from the ground. They hoped to find gold nuggets. When no gold was found, they said, "It didn't pan out." Now, it means 'Things did not go well.'

54. **It's raining cats and dogs.** To stay warm, in the olden days in Europe animals slept on the roofs of thatched houses, because the heat from inside warmed the roof. If it rained hard, they would fall off. Then, it would be 'raining cats and dogs.' Now, it means there is a heavy amount of rain.

55. **jay-walking**   'Jay' is a 19th century American term for an ignorant or provincial person who has not been to a city. Now, someone who does not obey traffic laws and crosses in the middle of the street, instead of at the corner, is 'jay-walking.'

56. **June bride**   In medieval England the first spring bath was in May. Clean for the first time in months, it was a good time for a girl to marry. So a "June bride" was nice, because she was clean.

57. **keep an eye out** Telescopes require one eye. In the days of sailing ships, sailors would say to their waiting families, "Keep an eye out for me." Now, it means, "Look for me."

58. **keep your shirt on** In the days of open-air boxing, if someone removed his shirt he was put in the ring to fight. Now it means 'wait a minute' or 'don't be in such a hurry.'

59. **let the cat out of the bag** In the Middle Ages in Europe, wandering merchants who sold rabbits would often try to cheat buyers by putting stray cats in tied bags instead of live rabbits. If careless, they would accidentally 'let the cat out of the bag' before they sold it. Then the buyer would learn the truth. Now, to 'let the cat out of the bag' means to accidentally tell the truth about something.

60. **mascot** From 13th century Gallia Narbonensis (France) a *mascotte* (sorcerer, or witch) helped someone win in gambling. Now, in sports, teams have their favorite animal that symbolizes the team, and they call it their 'mascot.'

61. **mausoleum** A stately burial tomb. Original massive marble tomb built for Persian satrap (governor) *Mausolos* by his wife Artemisia. Now, it's a beautiful little building to contain the corpse of someone who wants to pay for an expensive coffin.

62. **mind your p's and q's** In Britain the bartender would keep track of how many pints or quarts the customers drank, by writing on a chalkboard a 'p' (for pint) or a 'q' (for quart) in order to get correctly paid. If customers had too much to drink, their blurred vision made it difficult for them to see how much they had drunk – or to see if the bartender added to the bill without them knowing. Now, it means to pay careful attention to what you are doing.

63. **off the cuff** From the 1930s, when speakers or actors would secretly read from notes from the disposable paper cuffs of their

shirt sleeves. Now it means to give a speech without any preparation.

64. **on the hot seat**   In Medieval times, a suspect was placed on a metal seat of heated spikes until he confessed.   Now it means to be questioned.

65. **over a barrel**   The earliest known meaning (from Oxford English Dictionary) is a nearly drowned person, being rolled 'over a barrel' to force out the water. So, the nearly-drowned person was "over a barrel" and at the mercy of whoever would roll him. Now, to have someone 'over a barrel' means to have their fate in your hands.

66. **pass the buck**   In the era of the American Frontier, during poker games, a knife with a buckhorn (deer) handle was passed to the person whose responsibility it was to deal the cards. Now, "to pass the buck" to someone means the responsibility now belongs to that person.

67. **pay lip service** The expression dates back to the 1640s. Someone will make a promise (use one's lips) to do something, but not actually do anything. Now, 'to pay lip service' means that someone makes an empty promise to do something, and doesn't do it.

68. **pay through the nose** In 9th century Ireland the conquering Danes imposed an exorbitant nose tax (part of the census) threatening to put a knife 'through the nose' of those who did not pay. Now it means something is very expensive.

69. **pie in the sky**   Words in a 1911 song by an American labor leader, Joe Hill, seeking food for the hungry and the poor, and criticizing religious promises of heavenly rewards as 'pie in the sky.' Now, it means you are dreaming if you think some particular plan will work.

70. **pipe dreams** Pleasant dreams which people had when they smoked opium through a long pipe. Now it means someone is out of touch with reality, and is dreaming.

71. **piss poor** Originally urine was used to tan animal hides. If the only way a family could earn money was to collect their own urine in a pot and sell it to the leather company, they were 'piss poor.' Now it means someone is very poor.

72. **pull the wool over his eyes** Judges in British courts traditionally wore wool wigs. So, if a lawyer confused a judge, it was like pulling the wool (wig) over a judge's eyes so he could not see the truth. Now, it means to deceive someone.

73. **pulling your leg** This is probably from 19th century London. When thieves worked in pairs, one thief would trip a victim and pull his leg while pretending to help him – while the other would pick the victim's pockets. Now, it means to have fun and tease someone in a friendly way.

74. **read between the lines** For centuries, secret messages were written 'between the lines' of a letter, using milk or lemon juice. Recipients would heat the letter to 'read between the lines.' Now it means to find out what the truth really is.

75. **red-handed** Often people stealing and butchering someone's animals would have blood on their hands... and be 'caught red-handed.' Now it means someone is caught and has no excuse.

76. **saved by the bell** To aid people accidentally buried alive (before modern science), a bell was put on the outside of coffins with a string inside. If the person awoke, they could pull the string and be 'saved by the bell.' Now it means you were saved by something happening which you did not expect.

77. **saving face**   In the 18th century in Europe, women wore much make-up to impress everyone. Since they did not bathe often, the make-up became thicker and thicker. If they sat near a fire place, the heat would melt it and they would look terrible.   So they would have to leave, in order to 'save face.'   Now, it means that, to avoid looking stupid, someone will say or do something to 'save face.'

78. **scapegoat**   In *Leviticus 16:8* the sins of Israel were put on a goat sent into the wilderness. Now whoever is blamed for doing something bad is called the 'scapegoat.'

79. **scarce as hen's teeth**   It means 'very rare,' since most birds do not have teeth.

80. **second string**   When bows and arrows were an essential part of warfare, archers kept a 'second string' handy in case the first string broke or got wet. Now, it means a second group of athletes, who are not as qualified or as well-trained as the first group, but who will replace the first group when needed.

81. **send flowers**   Before embalming, friends of the deceased person often sent flowers to mask the odor of the decomposing body. It dates back to the Shanidar Caves in Iraq over 10,000 years ago. Now, to 'send flowers' means to express your best wishes.

82. **snob**   One explanation dates back to old England and prestigious schools, where the students wrote their noble family status or title on a certificate. If a student was not from the nobility, he would write *sine nobilitate,* meaning 'without nobility' – the abbreviation was 's.nob.' Because these students were from the lower class, they just pretended they were important. Now, a snob is someone who pretends to be more important than he or she really is.

83. **speak of the devil**   People once believed that the devil was inside of 'evil' people. Now, when a 'bad' person arrives people say, "Speak of the devil."

84. **start the ball rolling**   In the British sport of croquet, someone has to be the first one to hit the ball and start it rolling. Now, the expression means to start moving.

85. **steal someone's thunder**   In the 1700s, the English dramatist John Dennis invented a gadget to imitate thunder. When a rival producer used Mr. Dennis' sound effects for his own performances, Mr. Dennis was upset and said, "He's stealing my thunder." Now, it means someone is taking credit for what you said or did.

86. **stool pigeon**   To attract pigeons, hunters would tie a pigeon to a stool; its cry of alarm would attract other pigeons. Thus, the term 'stool pigeon' was regarded as a squealing traitor.

87. **strait-laced**   In 15th century England poem, ladies tied their dresses and corsets tight with lace (a nice string). Since they were 'strait-laced' they could not move freely. By the 16th century, it meant any people with rigid religious or moral beliefs who would not change their minds about anything. Now, it means someone who is very careful not to make a mistake in manners, morals, or opinions.

88. **T-shirt**   Simple shirt in the shape of a 'T' for a hot climate. Easy to clean, these shirts for hot climates were adopted by the US Navy during the Spanish-American War (1898).

89. **throw out the baby with the bath water.**   In the olden days, the man of the house bathed first, and then others took turns. The baby was the last person to get a bath, and so the water was very dirty. Therefore, someone might accidently "throw out the baby with the bath water." Now, it means, 'be careful not to throw good things out with bad things.'

90. **the pen is mightier than the sword**   An expression from an English author. It means you can be more powerful by what you write, than by hurting a few people with a physical weapon.

91. **tie the knot** In ancient times, the priest performing a wedding ceremony would tie the hands of the bride and groom together with rope. In modern times, in some ceremonies the priest will still put a sash around their hands instead of a rope, to show that the couple is about to 'tie the knot.'

92. **tip** In *Old Rogues Cant* (slang of thieves) in the 17th century, it meant 'to give or share' with someone who helped you. In modern times, some people say it's an abbreviation of "**T**o **I**nsure **P**romptness" (TIP) in order to get better service from a waiter or waitress. So, it is extra money you give to someone for their service, such as a waiter or waitress. (Or, it can also mean some advice you give to someone.)

93. **to the bitter end**   A 'bitt' is a post on the deck of a ship on which to fasten ropes or the anchor cable. The end of the rope which goes around the bitt inside of the boat is the 'bitter end.' So, 'to the bitter end' means you will be with someone together 'in the same boat' until the end.

94. **toe the line** In early 19th century England, competitors in a footrace were required to keep their front toe behind a 'line' or 'mark' to start the race.   Now, it means to 'stay honest and proper.'

95. **too many cooks spoil the soup** Many cooks will disagree about what should go into a soup. So, in life, if you get opinions from too many people, you may make the wrong decision.

96. **turnpike** In 17th century Middle English 'turnepike' was a spiked barrier on roads which prevented a vehicle from passing. After a fee was paid, the attendant 'turned' the 'pike' to allow traffic to pass. Now, it is a major highway with toll booths, in which you pay a fee.

97. **two wrongs don't make a right**   If someone does something bad to you, it doesn't help to do something wrong yourself. It doesn't make anything 'right,' but only makes things worse.

98. upper crust Workers and peasants got the burned bottom of a loaf of bread, the family got the middle, and important guests received "the upper crust" which was the most delicious part of the bread. Now, 'upper crust' refers to people who are wealthy.

99. wet your whistle It has meant to 'take a drink' since the 14th century in England. It refers to cleaning one's wind pipes, in order to whistle (essential for calling animals). Now, it means to take a drink of some kind of alcohol.

100.whistle blower In 1884, the police in London first used whistles to alert people of a problem. In the US, in the 1970s the consumer advocate Ralph Nader used the term to refer to someone inside of the government who alerts the public of something wrong inside of the government.

Answer Key

Words 1-5
c	(a) abduct
e	(b) accused
a	(c) accurate
b	(d) accumulate
d	(e) abandon

Words 6-10
c	(a) addiction
a	(b) adolescent
e	(c) acquire
b	(d) adapt
d	(e) adjacent

Words 11-15
b	(a) advocate
e	(b) adversary
a	(c) affluent
c	(d) affection
d	(e) aesthetic

Words 16-20
b	(a) allegiance
c	(b) aggravated
d	(c) agnostic
a	(d) allocate
e	(e) aggregate

Words 21-25
d	(a) amend
b	(b) ambidextrous
a	(c) ancestor
e	(d) analysis
c	(e) ambiguous

Words 26-30
c	(a) arrogance
d	(b) annex
a	(c) apprehend
e	(d) arbitrary
b	(e) anticipate

Words 31-35
b	(a) assess
d	(b) astronomy
a	(c) ascertain
e	(d) association
c	(e) assimilate

Words 36-40
c	(a) average
a	(b) autonomy
e	(c) authority
b	(d) aversion
d	(e) balance

Words 41-45
b	(a) biology
d	(b) blamed
a	(c) beautiful
e	(d) bibliography
c	(e) bias

Words 46-50
c	(a) burden
d	(b) boring
b	(c) bureaucracy
a	(d) bonfire
e	(e) boycott

Words 51-55
c	(a) candidate
b	(b) cast
a	(c) bury
e	(d) cartel
d	(e) candid

Words 56-60
b	(a) cause
d	(b) cease
a	(c) catastrophe
e	(d) certify
c	(e) characteristic

Words 61-65
b	(a) civil
c	(b) chronology
e	(c) choose
a	(d) coalition
d	(e) circulate

Words 66-70
b	(a) commodity
d	(b) collide
a	(c) cohesion
e	(d) coercion
c	(e) coincide

Words 71-75
a	(a) component
d	(b) compensate
b	(c) complicated
e	(d) complex
c	(e) compromise

Words 76-80
e	(a) conquer
b	(b) conflict
a	(c) confidence
c	(d) concentrate
d	(e) condemn

Words 81-85
b	(a) conscious
d	(b) constitution
a	(c) constraint
e	(d) consequences
c	(e) contaminate

Words 86-90
c	(a) contemplate
e	(b) contest
a	(c) contempt
b	(d) contrary
d	(e) context

Words 91-95
d	(a) convince
b	(b) convey
c	(c) core
a	(d) counter
e	(e) cultivate

Words 96-100
d	(a) December
e	(b) dedicate
c	(c) curriculum
a	(d) declined
b	(e) cynical

Words 101-105
c   (a) degrade
e   (b) delinquent
d   (c) demanded
a   (d) deduct
b   (e) deity

Words 106-110
c   (a) descendant
d   (b) denied
a   (c) demographics
e   (d) denote
b   (e) democracy

Words 111-115
b   (a) destination
c   (b) despondent
e   (c) detail
a   (d) designated
d   (e) despise

Words 116-120
c   (a) diagnosis
a   (b) dexterous
e   (c) dilemma
b   (d) detain
d   (e) devise

Words 121-125
a   (a) disease
e   (b) dire
b   (c) discreet
c   (d) discriminate
d   (e) diminish

Words 126-130
c   (a) disregard
a   (b) dismiss
e   (c) diverse
b   (d) distinct
d   (e) distort

Words 131-135
d   (a) domesticate
e   (b) dynamic
a   (c) elementary
b   (d) elite
c   (e) election

Words 136-140
d   (a) engender
a   (b) embrace
e   (c) enlighten
b   (d) enterprising
c   (e) emissions

Words 141-145
b   (a) entrepreneur
d   (b) equity
c   (c) erudite
e   (d) essential
a   (e) erode

Words 146-150
e   (a) exotic
d   (b) evidence
a   (c) evade
b   (d) evolution
c   (e) exclusive

Words 151-155
b   (a) expense
e   (b) experience
a   (c) expeditiously
c   (d) extend
d   (e) exploit

Words 156-160
c   (a) familiar
a   (b) extract
b   (c) extreme
e   (d) extinguish
d   (e) false

Words 161-165
c   (a) feasible
a   (b) famine
b   (c) fatal
e   (d) feature
d   (e) February

Words 166-170
b   (a) flood
e   (b) focus
a   (c) fertilize
c   (d) flourish
d   (e) fluctuate

Words 171-175
d   (a) folklore
e   (b) forensics
a   (c) formal
b   (d) forecast
c   (e) foil

Words 176-180
b   (a) foundation
e   (b) fortify
a   (c) function
c   (d) frequent
d   (e) furnish

Words 181-185
b   (a) gain
d   (b) gala
e   (c) futile
a   (d) gale
c   (e) gap

Words 186-190
b   (a) generation
e   (b) geology
a   (c) gender
c   (d) genuine
d   (e) govern

Words 191-195
c   (a) grotesque
a   (b) habitable
e   (c) guilty
b   (d) gut
d   (e) gratitude

Words 196-200
e   (a) hazardous
d   (b) harassed
a   (c) hallucinate
b   (d) hedonistic
c   (e) haggle

Words 201-205
e   (a) homogenous
d   (b) hilarious
a   (c) hierarchy
b   (d) honeymoon
c   (e) horror

Words 206-210
a   (a) hypocrite
e   (b) humiliated
d   (c) hover
b   (d) hydrated
c   (e) hypothesis

Words 211-215
c   (a) illiterate
e   (b) idealistic
a   (c) impact
b   (d) implement
d   (e) hysterical

Words 216-220
c   (a) impoverished
e   (b) improvise
a   (c) impulsive
b   (d) implicate
d   (e) implicit

Words 221-225
b   (a) inaugurate
e   (b) incoherent
a   (c) incompetent
c   (d) incentive
d   (e) incident

Words 226-230
b   (a) industrious
e   (b) indisputable
a   (c) infinitesimal
c   (d) inference
d   (e) indispensible

Words 231-235
e   (a) inflation
a   (b) inherent
d   (c) inherit
b   (d) ingenious
c   (e) influence

Words 236-240
b   (a) inquire
c   (b) innovate
e   (c) initiative
a   (d) inhibit
d   (e) inject

Words 241-245
e   (a) inscription
a   (b) innocent
c   (c) insight
b   (d) install
d   (e) integrate

Words 246-250
c   (a) intentional
e   (b) integrity
a   (c) intensify
d   (d) intercept
b   (e) interactive

Words 251-255

d   (a) intermediate
b   (b) intricate
a   (c) intervene
e   (d) interdict
c   (e) interface

Words 256-260

d   (a) intuition
a   (b) invade
b   (c) intrude
c   (d) intrinsic
e   (e) invalid

Words 261-265

b   (a) itinerary
c   (b) irrational
e   (c) invoke
a   (d) irrigate
d   (e) involved

Words 266-270

b   (a) juvenile
d   (b) jointly
c   (c) justify
a   (d) January
c   (e) journalism

Words 271-275

d   (a) karma
e   (b) kin
a   (c) Knowledge
b   (d) juxtapose
c   (e) lament

Words 276-280

c   (a) latitude
e   (b) lease
a   (c) latent
b   (d) legitimate
d   (e) legacy

Words 281-285

d   (a) liberal
c   (b) loyal
e   (c) liability
a   (d) lunatic
b   (e) luxury

Words 286-290

c   (a) malignant
d   (b) manipulate
a   (c) magnificent
e   (d) maintain
b   (e) marginal

Words 291-295

c   (a) maximize
a   (b)memorize
e   (c) masculine
b   (d) meditation
d   (e) merchant

Words 296-300

d   (a) migration
a   (b) milieu
e   (c) minimum
b   (d) milestone
c   (e) merit

Words 301-305
c   (a) modify
a   (b) motive
e   (c) mobilize
b   (d) multitude
d   (e) misconception

Words 306-310
e   (a) nightmare
c   (b) mutation
a   (c) mystery
b   (d) naive
d   (e) negligent

Words 311-315
d   (a) nobility
a   (b) nucleus
c   (c) notion
e   (d) novice
b   (e) November

Words 316-320
e   (a) obese
a   (b) obnoxious
d   (c) nutrition
b   (d) objectivity
c   (e) oath

Words 321-325
e   (a) obtain
a   (b) offenses
d   (c) obligation
b   (d) oligarchy
c   (e) October

Words 326-330
d   (a) oppress
c   (b) oppose
e   (c) overwhelm
a   (d) pacify
b   (e) oxygen

Words 331-335
c   (a) paradigm
a   (b) paradox
e   (c) panacea
b   (d) parallel
d   (e) pariah

Words 336-340
b   (a) passionate
c   (b) parochial
e   (c) per capita
a   (d) peers
d   (e) paternal

Words 341-345
e   (a) perspective
d   (b) persist
a   (c) perseverance
b   (d) permeated
c   (e) phantom

Words 346-350
d   (a) physical
a   (b) philosophy
e   (c) philanthropist
c   (d) phonetics
b   (e) photosynthesis

Words 351-355

c   (a) plunge
e   (b) plagiarizing
d   (c) plummet
a   (d) piracy
b   (e) pious

Words 356-360

e   (a) policy
a   (b) precedent
b   (c) potent
c   (d) poll
d   (e) portray

Words 361-365

b   (a) prejudice
c   (b) predicament
e   (c) prestige
a   (d) prescription
d   (e) pretended

Words 366-370

e   (a) privilege
a   (b) procedure
d   (c) procrastinated
b   (d) prognosis
c   (e) prevail

Words 371-375

a   (a) proportion
e   (b) proliferation
b   (c) promote
c   (d) proprietor
d   (e) prosper

Words 376-380

d   (a) proximity
e   (b) protruded
a   (c) quality
b   (d) prototype
c   (e) psychic

Words 381-385

c   (a) radical
a   (b) rate
e   (c) ratio
b   (d) quandary
d   (e) rank

Words 386-390

d   (a) recipient
e   (b) reciprocate
a   (c) rebel
b   (d) recede
c   (e) reconciliation

Words 391-395

d   (a) reform
a   (b) regulate
e   (c) rectified
b   (d) relic
c   (e) represent

Words 396-400

c   (a) reservoir
d   (b) residual
a   (c) resign
b   (d) resist
e   (e) resume

Words 401-405
d   (a) reward
c   (b) retrieve
e   (c) revolved
b   (d) rigor
a   (e) retain

Words 406-410
e   (a) sacrifice
a   (b) roster
b   (c) safeguard
c   (d) rotate
d   (e) ritual

Words 411-415
c   (a) scandal
d   (b) scar
a   (c) seize
e   (d) secular
b   (e) saga

Words 416-420
d   (a) September
b   (b) sequence
e   (c) severe
a   (d) shame
c   (e) sentiment

Words 421-425
c   (a) sibling
d   (b) shuttle
a   (c) significant
e   (d) shrink
b   (e) simulate

Words 426-430
d   (a) smuggle
e   (b) sole
a   (c) sincere
b   (d) sinister
c   (e) solar

Words 431-435
c   (a) spinster
e   (b) source
d   (c) spectrum
a   (d) solid
b   (e) stability

Words 436-440
d   (a) *status quo*
e   (b) strategy
a   (c) structure
b   (d) subsidize
c   (e) stigmatize

Words 441-445
e   (a) suspected
d   (b) surveillance
a   (c) suspend
c   (d) survive
b   (e) subtle

Words 446-450
d   (a) threshold
e   (b) tolerate
b   (c) symbol
c   (d) tangible
a   (e) terminate

Words 451-455

e	(a) universal
d	(b) understand
a	(c) trend
b	(d) ulterior
c	(e) trigger

Words 456-460

d	(a) versus
a	(b) utilize
e	(c) vanity
b	(d) verdict
c	(e) vanish

Words 461-465

d	(a) vestige
a	(b) voyage
b	(c) villain
e	(d) violate
c	(e) vitriolic

Words 466-470

d	(a) wound
b	(b) witness
e	(c) withdraw
c	(d) withhold
a	(e) vulnerable

Words 471-475

e	(a) zealous
d	(b) xenophile
a	(c) xenophobic
b	(d) zone
c	(e) yield

My English Notes

My English Notes

My English Notes

My English Notes

My English Notes

My English Notes

About the Authors

Charles W. Sutherland has studied a number of languages (Latin, Greek, German, French, Russian), including as a student at the University of Vienna (Austria) and at the *Institut Français VIllefranche-sur-Mer* (France), and is an author of numerous books.

Daniel C. Sutherland is a graduate of The College of William & Mary in Virginia, fluent in Spanish, and a former student at the *Universidad de Cádiz* (Spain) and the University of Nottingham (United Kingdom).

David Carter is Professor of Art, and former Chairman of the Art Department, of Montgomery College in Maryland.

Made in the USA
Middletown, DE
16 March 2023

26914373R00209